<u>Belonging</u>

Nick Clube

I come in peace,
With seedlings.
The earth drew me,
In green.

I grew from soil,
Between wars.
This world coloured me,
With dust.

The Peoples Poet

Anthology
2003

An anthology of new poetry
by the people for the people.

ISBN 0-9543621-0-1
First Edition

Published by Paula Brown Trading as The People's Poet

Printed in Great Britain by Antony Rowe Ltd
Chippenham Wiltshire

Contents

Introduction

The People's Poet is a new poetry project, created to publish talented poets at no cost to themselves.

The writers themselves have chosen the content of this anthology online, so this project has been purely poetry by the people for the people.

Undoubtedly, this project has uncovered much literary talent and has been the source of a wonderful poetic online community.

The Panel's involvement was created to ensure that not all of the work in this book was seen in advance by all of the poets and visitors to the site. Also, it gave the opportunity for writers to have fun creating a little section of their own favourites. This panel will change each year and anybody who has been an active part of this anthology project is eligible to apply to be on next year's panel.

The content of this anthology is diverse in style and length, from a little verse to an entire Epic but you can be sure that every work within these pages has moved several readers to pass comment and vote for that piece to be included.

Please look out for the competitions at the back of this book, and the voting form for the Peoples Poet 2003. Anybody purchasing a copy of this book is eligible to enter any or all of these competitions.

And finally, many thanks to everyone who has been a part of this project, enabling it to grow to become such a great success.

Paula Brown (nee Cleife)

The Peoples Poet Panel Selections

Dave Brown

        Paula Cleife

Dave Seaman

          Karl Graham

       Sarah Tracy

                Ade Rowley

         Pete Bishop

              Pete Nightingale

Dave Brown

I am 34 and from Dorset.
I am pleased to be a member of this year's panel because
I enjoy reading and writing straight-talking poetry. Here are a couple of mine.

SANTA POD

Eight jets of fire, burning;
Five thousand horses, pounding.
Ten thousand eyes, watching
Two men whose hearts are racing.

Lights turn red to green;
Fire burns, horses scream.
Rubber smokes, a winning team.
Five seconds to a dream.

STASIS LEAK

To be chlorescent but not to feel
Indolescent in the last;
To win the truth and yet to fail
My violaceous vast.
If seeing is believing this,
You'll say I'm there too fast.
But I win the aim and lose again:
I'm living in the past.

Dave Brown's Selection

DO I STILL WOO MY WIFE??

John J Whitmarsh (Married, with black eyes!)

(Paula asked me if I wooed my wife that way!)

I discovered something strange today –
No, more than strange, quite weird, in fact –
Concerning things I do and don't,
Things that I forget to do,
And one of these
(I swear it's true!)
Is that I never
Bother
Woo
The one
I really ought to woo!

I woo the rest,
It's second nature –
Women are my hobby, yet
Although I email scores each day,
And dream up a thousand things to say
To win their hearts and earn their smiles,
I never pay such rich attention
(Or hardly ever bother mention)
My feelings for the woman who
Was the first that I did woo –
Amends are called for,
And I will do
This for
My antique wife
(Called Sue)

As soon as all the kids are gone
I'll set my wooer's mind upon
Words and jokes and poetry
To win the heart
That belongs to me!

But wooing one whose known me use
Every tried and tested ruse
On a thousand girls before
Is harder than it ought to be –
The problem with it all, she says,
Is that she spends her holidays
Reading through my private mails;
So, you see, she knows the tales
And all the ditties, rhymes and jokes
That I use on other folks.
It's hopeless offering second-hand woos –
And these are all I have to use –
So I'll resort to subtler ways:

I'll stroke her hair and rub her back
And tell her that she's not TOO fat,
And say I'm tired and want to rest
And ask her if it's time for bed –
And then, dear reader,
You will agree
The ending is not for you to see –
Surely you will not intrude
On something that is
REALLY
Wooed!

Silent Mystery
Thomas Moore

The brain is dead inside my head
has been for years,
No feeling for the summer, or
sight, for the glint on
the river, relieved of
responsibility? morality?
An ache inside my chest
panic, move to safety,
relief. Then Silence.
not silence but Silence.
Not of the grave,
but the quietness
that follows conception.

In fifteen minutes a
light year passes then
conscious knowledge
but different.
Strange new voice,
familiar place but, different?

They? said it was "near death"
but I knew, they were wrong.
I knew.
Now? I am different, alive,
in control, no fear, no panic,
ever again, at last I know
the meaning and
there is only conception.

Last Night For A Verse
Miguel Angel Berrios

And life fades away,
As I touch you,
I feel that your heart is an echo of me.
Meaningless, what I say,
When even poets die
With their best words unsaid.

Just like me,
With a lifetime of nights by your side
And tonight,
That I wanted to tell you, my love,
I just said good-bye.

Extremes
Karl Graham

Springing out of bed/Been in bed for 14 hours
With hope and joy in my mind/Not getting up "Why should I?"
Quickly dressed, washed and out the door/Pull my head back under the covers
Heading for the river "What will I find?"/And I continue to cry
Next doors dog rushes by/My head's all messed up
To chase the stick I've just thrown/Nothing makes sense at all
All seems so still, nothing moving/Feels like I'm on a 1sq foot of ground
But I know we are not alone/Surrounded by a million mile high wall
The rush of life and survival/The phone rings then a knock at the door
In the sky and beneath my feet/People around me with love to give
I stop, look around and smile/"Leave me alone, go away, I don't want it"
LIFE! It cannot be beat/Then the thought forms "I don't want to live"

I DID MY BIT!
Sarah Tracy

I painted the walls a beautiful green
To keep my family nice and serene
I didn't like gardening, not very much
But I planted a tiny, neat little bush!
I saved all the paper, the cans and the glass
I even said a few prayers at mass
I didn't eat Tuna, felt sad for the whale
And cheered for Greenpaece, when off they'd sail
So why am I struggling for water and air?
And why is the land so scorched and bare?
Why did it happen? I tried my best
So I didn't begin as soon as the rest!
But they are all dying the same as me
So did it matter about the trees
Was it only the poisons - or greed as well
That turned our earth into living hell

Not Wordsworth
Samantha Jones

I wandered lonely as a cloud
How lonely can you get
I didn't wander quick enough
So I got soaking wet
I couldn't see a blessed thing
The rain bunged up me specs
Sod those bloody daffodils
I tripped and broke me neck

Robin's Arrow
Steve Todd

Where grace low-lieth, leave me there to die.
Where truth will always slay the duelling lie,
And roses live, and harvests never fail.
Wake wisdom up, entreat him weave a tale
To span these aeons. Paint the man I was;
Tell them, 'Waste you no time nor breath, because
The flesh and blood is fleeting, passing by'.
Where grace low-lieth, leave me there to die.

Where grace low-lieth, leave me there to die.
Where rolling hills of plenty siege the eye,
Where doubts but doubt themselves, and love remains
Spread from strong hearts to fill my failing veins.
Where social fetters bind my hands no more,
And Peace sleeps soundly, free from dreams of War.
The last breath should be one contented sigh-
Where grace low-lieth, leave me there to die.

Where grace low-lieth, leave me there to die.
Where horizons of azure brace the sky...
My memories blaze and set this mind alight!
For all your tears that douse them feed, not fight
The ancient hearth-flame dwindling in my breast
That kept me warm throughout the epic test.
Dear friends, you speak of Life! But so do I.
Where grace low-lieth, leave me there to die.

Not Tonight
Paula Cleife

Not tonight,
While the rain-kissed orchid
Aroma of your breath stings my nose.

Not tonight,
While I remember how we curled up
Like ringlets in a little girl's hair.

Not tonight,
While my fingertips still tremble
At the idea of your cotton-fresh,
Pillow-soft skin.

Not tonight,
While I am still thinking of what might have been.
I'll call you tomorrow,
But please.....

Not tonight.

how time flies
Andrew Penland

I watched a clock
(as gray a gravedigger's frock
coat) cease to tick,

grin cheshirely,
and float slowly
away.

(It had learned
to escape
by watching worms burrow

and doing the opposite
of what they do.)

My Russian Friend
Ricky Kane

When I'm with my Russian Friend
I'm on top of the world.
He shines upon me his sweet sophistication, creating
In myself a glowing beacon of confidence:
Courage. Charisma.

Since I've been playing with my Russian Friend
I've matured.
I can feel my inners ageing against time at triple rate,
With my outers bearing the glamour of being grown up:
Grey. Gaunt.

My other friends don't like my Russian Friend
(my old friends).
They say he's a bad influence, but since his introduction,
I've been influxed with a new wave of dreams. Who needs:
People. Prospects?

My Doctor wont let me play with my Russian Friend.
He's jealous.
I can't think of anyone, with whom I'd rather spend the afternoon,
Socialising through seductive sips; relaxing and reflecting with red:
Warm. Worldly.

My Russian Friend has had me and now left me
in the gutter.
My friends (my real friends) have gone and my doctor was right.
My mind has packed up and left with the bottle. My eyes as red as hell:
Where I'm headed.

Midsummer in Porkenas
Andy Saunders

Set and leave the shadows dance
Flickering low across the lake.
The noble trees cast patterns now
As if for beauty's sake.

Bright, so bright; the clouds they burn
Tear holes in the canvas of the sky.
Each ripple of the sea shines light
Reflections in them lie.

Light as day, yet dark as night,
Peculiar twilight time.
The magnificence of being part
Of nature's surreal rhyme.

Spectrum of the changing light
Torn, misty clouds drift high.
Each wash against the sand so dark,
A universal sigh!

It's never really dark here,
Yet dappled patterns play
As if the night is scared to show
Against everlasting day.

ALL IT TAKES IS A BEER
Karl Graham

Apprehension as usual when I arrive in a new place.
Will they dislike me? Or will they accept a new face?
Bags unpacked, out of the hostel, it is then that I see,
That men, women and children are no different than me.
Find a bar or a pub, that is my first aim,
With a few pints in side me, I then have no shame.
Now my neurons are suppressed I wander free, unlike I did,
My soul comes to the fore and out yet again comes the kid.
And as I run around this city with the child in my eyes,
I don't see enough, experience enough because time it just flies.

Reality beckons. I must put away the child at last
Because now it is time for me to leave this city of Belfast.

THREE WISHES

Jörgen Jansson

I've been viewing the insincere location below
I've been walking the roof of the flaming chaos
My endowments lay beyond the sceptic mind
The sanctuary has been the strength in silence

Inside the one dazzling light there's a wonderful voice
It's the answer to the million peoples three wishes
Freedom is the chorus for those who dared to die
Three wishes will be fulfilled, the light deliver the... dream

I know what will liberate, I understand the spirit
I never claimed to be the one superior prophet
All I want to is to convey the message of light
The deprived souls will no longer be the victims

Inside the one dazzling light there's a wonderful voice
It's a tune that holds the million peoples three wishes
It contains all the love for those who dared to die
Three wishes will be fulfilled, the light deliver the... dream

Things I've seen could never happen in understanding
The scared ignorant thieves of love, they thrash it all
The commandments? Broken, can't see the new one's
Hope love and empathy no longer follow hand in hand

Live love and learn - wishes builds your world up
You've got to learn how to live, follow your mind
You've got to live for love, be gentle and kind
You've got to love to learn to live, to share to give

Inside your own dazzling light there's a wonderful voice
It's a tune that holds the million peoples three wishes
It contains all the love for those who dared to die
Three wishes will be fulfilled, the light deliver the... dream

Am I Alone In Thinking This?
Geoff Hough 2002

They all fight for God, they do:
Moslem, Hindu, Christian, Jew,
He is always on 'their' side,
To justify their Genocide.
The common people sent to war,
To die like dogs upon the floor
Are His own chosen sons,
Sent by His elected ones.
If God is merciful and just:
-Why this awful bloody lust?
If his Son was meek and mild:
-Why kill another's tiny child?

And when the battle has been won,
The foe been vanquished, job well done.
The Generals, priests and Holy Men
Troop to church and temple then.
To give thanks to 'their' God
- It's this that strikes me - very odd!

Suicide Note
Ricky Kane

The chair creaks under my strain
I creak under my strain

So this is how it's going to end...
A rope - with me at the end.

Like your Grip, the rope suffocates and smoulders my neck,
Like your Poison, the rope has only one purpose at this point,
Like your Hate, the rope wants to see me suffer.

Like your Hold, the chair comforts me in my hour of need,
Like your Humour, the purpose of the chair is to keep me high,
Like your Love, the chair is solid - there to support me and keep me going.

Now you have gone, the chair too must go.
The Hate remains - The Rope remains - I am left to dangle.

DO TRAFFIC LIGHTS
Andrew Penland

do traffic lights
envy the voices of
rainbows? do pianos
blush when lovingly
touched? are abandoned houses
haunted by dreams?
does a cat worry if this life is his 9th?
do newspapers know when
their time is past? do dandelions
worry about coming apart? what if
raindrops are afraid to fall? do caterpillars
know their destiny (do butterflies
remember what they once were?)?

The Poet's Heart
Gareth Smith

When my skies turn black,
And the clouds hold sway,
My heart will fade out,
As my sun gives way.

When my sun creeps back,
And my skies turn blue,
My smile will return,
All shining, all new.

When my heart implodes,
And my landscape's dark,
There's nothing within,
No power, no spark.

When light leaves my life,
And I fall apart,
I suffer the curse,
Of the poet's heart.

Woman
Amy Baldry

Woman
Is not housekeeper
She is not wife nor mother
She is beauty

Alone she stands
As strong as oak
As soft as sand
Wind fraught flowers

The body gives
But the mind won't
She carries her heart
Like the thirsty carry water

Woman
Is not of one rib
She is not other nor opposite
She is beauty

Brave she stands
But concealed behind smiles
Her sorrow lives
But only in her eyes

Her light
Is like the sun's
Burning from within
Unreflecting

Woman
Is not silent
She is not invisible nor passive
She screams

Barefoot
She walks
Cut, bruised and tired
She walks on

After A Dream

John Whitmarsh

They gave me a gag, those moralists
They told me I must not speak:
They said those things should be taboo,
They said I should never care for you
The girl from Crocodile Creek.

"It is wrong," they said, those masters
"There are things you must not say."
They said "She will never understand."
They said "She will never hold your hand,"
The girl from so far away.

But I don't care for their restrictions
I can rise above them all:
So if I close my eyes and dream awhile,
Will you close yours too and see my smile
Green eyes, will you hear my call?

I will not be gagged by those moralists
I have words I cannot but speak:
I say, for me, there exists no taboo
That will stop my soul from telling you
My heart is in Crocodile Creek.

The Chancellor's Budget Speech.
John J Whitmarsh

I
Could
Build a
Mountain
From the lives
I have destroyed today.
In my name, babies will die;
Because of me, old men are broken,
Women lay on their backs in fear and agony,
And millions see the future as a lightless tunnel –
And all because of me, and the mountain of bright bullion
Sitting in the temple of our modern-day God – in the Treasury.

I
Call
This mountain
Cautious economy! And I
Commend this budget to the House.

Paula Cleife

Creator of The Peoples Poet.
I will be on the panel each year, and will be responsible
for the day-to-day running of the business.
I am 32, and from Dorset.
My own poetry page is at
http://paulaspoems.freeservers.com

THE ARTIST

The Artist moves his fingers across
The skin-smooth body of his work
As though it were a woman.
Is he caressing the curves
Or feeling for imperfections?

Intelligent, his mind is agile,
Like his body, moving deftly.
An adjustment here,
A finishing touch there.

The creation lives in his ideas
Until the day it is ready for display.
It suggests itself as he works,
One line draws him to another.

He is captivated by this.
Driven, even.

He will not rest until he is able
To rest his gaze on the glossy beauty,
Slip inside to feel the
Heartbeat of a new life.

The Artist has taken something ordinary
And made it beautiful.

TRAVELLING COMPANIONS

Our paths crossed;
We walked together awhile
Hand in hand
And then we realized in a teardrop
That we were each going
To a different place.
So we kissed our goodbyes
And continued on our way.

Paula's Selection

SING TO ME
Ade Rowley

I am not allowed to publish this one, but it is my favourite, nonetheless ☺

Question?
Dave Brown

If madness is viewed by
One who is not so;
Can he truthfully say that
An illness exists?
For this may be a balance:
An expression of feeling
Against those who are boring
And lacking in spirit

Patricia
John J Whitmarsh

Before her, black save for the steady light so far ahead,
Her private Via Dolorosa,
Cobbled in thorns,
Deep-littered with mantraps
And seeded with snares
Secreted within the trappings of everyday life ñ

But she, with her torch of Faith
And her Biblical map,
Wraps the cloak of Divine comfort
Tight about her fragile shoulders
And, with unflagging devotion,
Sets out to win the ultimate victory.

A RODDERS POEM

Lee Stevenson

The first time I saw you,
you were just a dream in my head,
a simple possibilty, an idea,
that kept me awake in my bed.

Now you're all finished,
and I have time to recall,
like the time your gearbox,
fell off its stand, and pinned me to the floor.

When your axles, diff and engine,
were lowered into your frame,
and I finally got your steering to work,
I was smug, never to be the same.

And as the cost mounted up,
and I gave the credit card some welly.
You always got the best I could afford,
Christ I nearly sold the telly.

Remember the time for the electrics,
there was a sleepless night or two,
Why won`t the f**king lights work,
oh sh*t a black to a blue.

Paint colour now fill my thoughts,
hummm, a shade of green, blue or red.
As I turn blankly at my partner,
Who`s screaming "DID YOU HEAR WHAT I JUST SAID!"

Driving home from the MOT station,
didn`t matter, rich or poor,
With a pass certificate in my hand,
I was the king of them all.

On the road, on my way to a show,
I`ve got people enviously looking at you,
I hear you engine burble and think,
It was worth twice the hassle, of what I went through.

So please God look down,
and send us some sunshine,
Because we all know,
that God drives a pre '49........

The Speechless Suitor

David W. Niewoehner

Ode to be, this is a dream.
With her, my heart pounds.

To taste those sweet moments that surround her,
With reverent calm, I beseech.

Unto deafness, my words fall,
For they, WERE NEVER SPOKEN !

Oh Cirano, WHERE ART THOU ?!
Why does my tongue weigh so much?

I wish, no pray!
End my torment and take my heart!

Alas, I am but a shadow, something
Without substance to her.

My wealth, for a moment of speech.
My life, for her adoration!

To this my faithful Bards, I SWEAR!
Take me, unto her heart.

Feed me to this bountifully beautiful maiden,
And I will be your man for life.

But alas, There is no hope, I'm told.
It's just a heart-felt jest.

She is of the Noble's tree,
And I, Just an oak.

Once

David Pert

I had this perfect dream,
Of lavender and painted roses,
Of sweet smelling warmth,
And thick velvet air,
That when pushed aside,
To let you by,
Spoke softly to my heart.

ALDEBURGH
David Savoury

The grey sea on the shingle sang
my summer's cooling silver
light on tides that, turning, foamed
grubby sand on stone.

Fishing-smacks that snugged the beach
blacked the chilly shore's
etiolated boomerang.
No gulls cried, people ate

fish and chips. They sat on walls
grey as the solid sea.
The pretty houses' windows looked
resigned to their exposure.

I drove to Snape, to catch a sense
of Britten. Beds of reeds,
dense and silent, choked the stream.
Strings of folk drank tea.

The cottage smelt of smoke: log fires
where others had been happy.
I turned the television on:
Russia had gone bankrupt.

Somewhere in the dark, the tide
withdrew; the pebbled beach
was strewn with refuse from a past
that foundered in its storm.

- Clouds -
Hugh D. Loxdale

Grey white, surreal, fantastic,
Light as cotton,
They scud, half-hearted, across the sky,
More intent on hiding the Sun
Than roving eastwards,
They deny its warmth
To us.
Breaking at their radiant edge
To shear into smaller and smaller   fragments,
Seeming to rotate,
            Yet in layers stacked,
Round and slowly round
They go,
Evaporating, trailing, tearing
Until even the very wisps
Disappear to leave...
Nothing but azure....
And the Sun's disc,
As pure bright,
Unforgiving as before,
We watch, full prone,
Our heads nesting on the ling
As the clouds,
Silent bring...
Their load of tears...
And cry freely on the fragile land..
Before moving off...
And out to sea.

Written on the Island of Sylt,
north Germany,
1st August, 2001

Distinguish my Soul
Karl Devitt

Drawn deep from my feet
Air so complete
Muscles like concrete.
Focussed mind
Pressures grind
Energies defined.
Channel open
Symphonies chosen
Silently broken
Cascading and bubbling
Power exploding
Stretching, imploding
Gasping and gulping
Mind golden
Dull ache
Forcefully revitalised
Singular and awesome.

THE LIVING DEAD
Sarah Tracy

Have you walked among the living dead
With demons of coldness in your head?
Did the monster, bitterness, gnaw at your face
Leaving hate in your heart for the human race?
Was the numbness a gift of peace or pain?
When it left did you go through it all again?
Only then did you weep, even more forlorn
For the joys of this world that had turned to stone.
Was it then that a song was hard to hear?
Was it even harder to shed a tear?
Did love seem a monster who kills and maims?
Did you ever think you would love again?
But take heart those of you who weep for your soul
Let yourself heal within and true love be your goal
For the thing that you lost was only your pride
And the gift that you gain is the love that's inside
So throw open your hearts and let love show
That hate, not man, is your greatest foe
And that love is never a waste of time
If it comes from within, it is divine

Goodbye Old Friend!!
Christopher Michael Palmer

I stand-alone with the breeze gently caressing my face,
I look out across the ocean as I stare in silence,
The grass of the high cliff top wet beneath my feet,
I try to reason, but find no answers within.

I wrap my arms around myself and close my eyes,
I drift off in to loneliness and silence of despair,
I hug you tight with my big strong arms,
Then a tear breaks free and rolls down my cheek.

I hold this repose, screwing my eyes up tight,
Then let out a sigh as my breath hangs on stilled night,
I slowly open my arms and beckon you near,
Then open my eyes and realize you are not here.

Many a night have I stood upon this cliff,
Just watching the rolling waves out on the bay,
I look within and find peace at last,
Then turn from the sea, this night will be my last!

KISS THE BOYS
Miguel Angel

Why would a boy in his innocence
kiss in the lips, younger boys.
Should he walk down the street, in no danger
should he play like those, with them, toys.

If an instant is not enough to anger
the weak of heart who performs,
lonely acts of desperate sadness
when I kiss the boys, in return.

Everyday there is nonsense, when spoken
words that are not to be true.
There are girls as available answers
but it is boys, that I kissed as I grew.

And I kiss the boys in their sadness,
kiss the boys in my room.
There are girls as available moments,
but it is boys, that I kissed as I grew.

Ghost
John Jones

This stifled life, the earthly price that fate would have me pay
Has stole from me, those tender words that love would have me say
So one day when my life is spent and my spirit free once more
I will shout out from the highest sky and you will hear my roar

For my ghostly air will ride the winds and seek your loving ear
And speak to you with loves true voice and you will feel me near
For without the twisting, turning knots that bind me to this place
I will cover you, and smother you in my heavenly embrace

ONE TO TREE
Karl Graham

TICK....................

Do you see me,hear me?
Perhaps while I sleep
Beneath arms so old
Ever skyward they creep.
Many wives you must have had
With all those rings around your core,
A polygamist most definitely
For my sake I hope there's more.

Strength is your asset
Against heat,wind and snow,
All year you must fight them,
In Spring,you defeat them and grow.
You set my imagination racing
And for your beauty I'll hew,
Much that it saddens me greatly
You may not see your life through.

TOCK....................
GOES THE TREE'S CLOCK

No Claim to Fame
Samantha Jones

I'm bored to tears, where is my fame
"It's overdue", I cry
I wanna see my name in lights,
In letters six feet high
I wanna be on Wogan's show
Jay Leno's would be nice
Instead of strugglin'with me work
And turning toward vice
To supplement the income
Pay the gas and phone
The listening bank 'ave all gone deaf
They won't give me a loan
I've sent it all to Parky
Some to the B.B.C
But I think they've all gone out
'cause no-one writes to me
To tell me I'll be famous
My work will be a hit
They only write to tell me
"Stop sending us this shit"!

Money
Sam Smith

Children want to believe in magic.
Sent upstairs
into the dark brown of Crosse House,
past the black linen-chest, below oil-thick paintings,
past the moving door of the slatted airing cupboard
its squatting tank and monstrous gaspings
lived Aunty in her narrow room.
From out of her black drapes came a long white hand,
with a whispered croak a silver threepenny bit
was placed in my palm.
I paid in politeness, then ran
down to Mrs Bakers, turned the threepence into a chew
and a rubbery zig-zag balloon.

In the grey stone wall on School Hill
were square drainage holes, child's height;
and in the crumbly soil at back of each,
an arm's reach for Brenda Collins and I,
we found sixpences and hexagonal threepenny bits.
Not every day.
So we always had to look, but kept it
secret, suspected kind fairies or crafty witches;
and exquisitely fearful, expecting any moment
to be turned into frogs,
we converted the money at top shop into sweets.

When I ran down the hill to the shops,
memorising the list, my mother let me sometimes
keep the change. Money in my pocket though
had a leper's bell jingle, So I threw the coppers
zinging along hot tarmac, snick-snicking
into hedgerow leaves, thudding off trunks.
To be found by a labourer digging or
a child looking at the small things.
Me,
Me the magician.

Dark And Strange
Chris Davies

I weave my way through the poem
Time and time again, trying hard
To click, clamber on, desperate;
 Tripping over dead bodies.

The dead bodies of great poets.
I stumble over the pale corpses,
 Shaking each by the collar,
'Show me the way, show me the way.'

But the strengthless face averts its eyes,
Unwilling to look at me, acknowledge,
 And I wander on alone, in the
Misty and dark anarchic graveyard.

Treasured words, loved by the world,
 But I do not see the light;
 The shiny little letters,
They are all dark and strange to me.

Chris tragically died in January 2001 as the result of a motor accident the previous Boxing Day. He was eighteen at the time, wrote poetry, songs and music, and this is an example of the remarkable talent which Chris had for words; a talent which was flowering, And which was stolen away.
I was lucky to have corresponded with him.
Peter Nightingale – April 2002.

The Old Man At The Bar

Nigel Spriggs

Saturday drifted by him
Sunday, he slept late
Read the papers - didn't think
What's to think of
Since you fell backwards
Loose limbed. Smiling.
Lost the focus in your eyes
Your death? Your syringes?
Your debts, which he has paid?
Nothing. It's too easy
To blur the ink from distant lives
To drift here Monday mornings
Eke out narrow life
Swill out stagnant mouthfuls
From the bottom of a glass
Balanced on a bar stool
Life's a balancing act
He remembers
You. A baby. Balanced on his knee
He remembers
You. In everything
Every little moment
Every little thing
You. Your thumb curled picture
Beside an empty glass of Stout

Blackpool Rock

Peter Nightingale

When I die,
Doctors will discover,
During the post-mortem,
That each segment of my body
Has your name, etched
In capitals, at its core.

Embedded in my bones,
Imprinted deep within
The nucleus of each dissected tissue,
In every molecule of every fibre,
Are letters spelling out
My reason for having been alive.

Voyage of the Lost

Geoff Hough

Textured twilight brings on the settled night,
The morning's bluster fades into noon's cat quietness and beyond.
City people, unbowed yet broken, find suburbia beckons,
Their snaking cars crawl, near stillborn,
Home to red-bricked havens, home to mortgaged dreams,
But hollow to youth's truths of yesteryear.
Does times tedium -crowned in a lilac fog -weigh heavy?
Do they airily reflect on futures fair or passions past?
Or does dreams despair sit deadweight on the chest?

Back to.....
Long, hot Sixties summers blazed in modern newness,
Reaching gaudily out from those stark monochrome years,
Tendrils fresh and searching, seeking out the tired past.
White hot heat, rhythm and blues, little red books,
Purple Hazes and Yellow Submarines,
Crashing together in a symphony of psychedelia.
Gone were little adults, youth was King Triumphant, youth was everything.

Fast forward.....
Retirements sweet repose, years of deskbound toil relented,
Pensioned safe, your deeds cemented.
Holiday sagas, bridge club parties, garden galas.
And yet did you tread youth's dream laid path?
Have you built your brave new world?
Imaginings lost in life's morass.

Fast reverse....
Music's universal torch in those pure fields of summer.
Youth's amity shone ever bright and free.
Challenge to accepted order, no tired suits, no national border.
Dylan at the Isle of Wight, or Woodstock's glowing beacon light,
Fired and furnaced youths new turning chapter.

Pause.
Don't forget the bedroom paint,
Or Tuesday's so important dinner date.
Should I wear the blue serge suit?
Will the wife serve cream with fruit?

Reverse........
Che and Mao, Leon and Lenin, sainted icons, heralds of Red Victory,
Prophets to Capitals oracled demise.
Demonstrations, remonstrations,
Sit-ins, love -ins, lock -outs.
You the vanguard of life's new order,
The shining seer of bright Arcadia,
Before your dreams were broke upon life's bitter rack.

Forward again.....
You meet a girl, a special one,
Your dreams turn back burned on the shelf as you serve your human self.
Love, libido, family matters, before you know they're torn and tattered.
Is this the poison point of innocence's loss?
Reactions counterattacking thrust?

And the music changed.....
Pistolled punks and disco hunks, New Romantics but the same old Antics.
Factory churnings and dollar earnings, Midas souls for cynical songsters.
Reverse....
The Sixty's golden glow dims to Seventies embered time.
Fusion, disillusion, Uncle Sam and Vietnam,
Abuse of powers, atomic towers, Three-day weeks and deep throat leaks,
- The old besieged by embryonic new.
And everyone, including you, had a point of view.

Forward....
You buy a house, your stake in life - a home for the kids, the car, the wife.
Bricks and mortar, a son, two daughters.
Wrapped up in now, forgetting how you dreamed of a different world.
A world for all, a world at peace - instead a mortgage and extended lease.

Pause.
This cars nearly three years old,
Think I'm starting with a cold.
What disc should I play next?
Another beep, another text.

Fast Forward....
The past reforms, reaction dawns, returning the stifled nights of years ago.
Out goes Keynes with your stolen dreams as you consume in a retailed hell.
Tax cut votes, stock market floats,
Credit cards and security guards,
Scrap heaped workers, the social shirkers.
But your all right -you've got your piece of the pie.

And the music changed........
Rolling Stones in stately homes and tired old Faces in exotic places.
Designer groups and megastars, Indy bands but fast new cars.

Play......
Sixties youth comes of age, they take the set, take the stage,
Now's their chance for a new world order,
No more want, no more murder.
But they've all been on the self same journey,
The voyage of the lost, compromised really.
How can we expect that dream in truth,
From those halcyon days of our golden youth?

Textured twilight brings on the settled night,
The evening fades into a melancholic blackness.
Their cars, purring effortlessly, mount suburban drives,
Headlamps, highlighting dreams out of the seeping dark,
Hollow, saccharine, ersatz dreams.....

Karl Graham

I was always the scientific one and left the creativity to my father and sister until I became diabetic in 1996. This opened a whole new and wonderful part of my mind, which allows me to sculpt, paint and write. My poetry is mainly about the beauty and at the same time the sadness of what I see and feel. To see my work please visit http://www.sunsetchaser.freeservers.com

HEY, GOOD TO SEE YOU AGAIN

Hey, good to see you again,
Gosh it must be almost a year.
Where've you been? What have you been up to?
You've been over the Atlantic I hear.

It was a shame about your parents dying
But I'm sure they'd be proud of you.
You've come back to the place of your birth
To make sure your genes carry through.

I hope your life turns out like you want it,
I hope you get what you strive for in your heart.
Life's a struggle and I see that you prove that.
But now it is time for me to depart.

And as I walk tearfully away from the waterfall,
It's good to see the salmon jumping again.

Karl's Selections

WORTH REPEATING
Paul Allan White

I loathe and despise you
Never ever said I liked you
See what's bad
and what's worse
is that sadness inside you

I just can't understand you
There's no-one quite like you

I dislike you intensely
I intensely dislike you

<u>Forgotten How to be me</u>

Alan Connor 2000

I shut my heart in a prison,
For which there was only one key,

She locked the door on my heart,
Ensured I could never be free,

She bound me to her forever,
Vowed her love for me would last,

But now dark days are upon me,
As my love lies trapped in the past,

Onward and forward forever,
Seems to be her battle cry today,

Get on with your life stop moping,
She tells me in every way,

She can't stop my tears from flowing,
She's not here to help with the pain,

Yet I find it so easy to forgive her,
For I need her to be mine once again.

I still want to stay in my prison,
So cosy as she holds the key,

But she is forcing me into daylight,
She is trying to set me free,

I'm sorry my love I don't want to,
Please don't tell me I've got to be free,

Please don't open the door of my prison,
I've forgotten how to be me.

IF I COULD.....

Tanya Persson

If I could look at my dreams, through the mirror of belief,
And my life, through the mirror of self worth...
I would spread my wings, over the raging fire
With confidence that it would not burn, but carry me higher

I've been promised that somewhere on Earth
The stars meet the ocean, and Heaven gives birth,
To a place where waves crash silently to shore,
And where the mermaids dance as the eagles soar

If I could look at this Earth, through the mirror of acceptance
And the Universe, through the mirror of truth...
I would climb the highest mountains, scream out my frustrations
And smile at the thought of this blessed creation

If I could look at you, through the mirror of fate
And your soul, through the mirror of dreams...
I would lay to rest my desires, accept defeat in this fight
And watch, as your spirit sets the world alight

I've been promised that somewhere on Earth
The stars meet the ocean, and Heaven gives birth,
To a place where waves crash silently to shore,
And where the mermaids dance as the eagles soar.

Where Do I Go From Here?

Dave Seaman

How do I take that small step
that seems a light-year away?
How can I make that split-second decision
that takes forever and a day?
When does a friendship
turn into a relationship?
When does someone to whom you're like a brother
suddenly turn out to be your dream-lover?
Why am I so confused,
feel so discarded and used,
broken and abused
like a plug that's been fused?
I feel untrue to myself,
not to mention to my friend...
A friendship so valuable,
I would die were it to end.
If I ever needed inspiration
then that time is now;
but even if it came, I know
I'd still be at a loss for words, somehow.
I think I just have to face the fact
that I'm really in a mess.
It's not the way I wanted things,
but I'll live with it. (I guess.)
I've come so far, yet lost so much ground;
I don't know what to do.
The solution is somewhere lying around...
But I never thought the problem would be you.

I LEFT YOU
Paula Cleife

When we first spoke, my darling, you blew hotter than the sun.
Dazzled by your inimitable verve and sense of fun.
We kissed: oh wow! The fireworks exploded on my tongue.
I believed that I could love you, you could be the only one.

But summer turned to winter and your heart a cooling blue.
Secluded in your solitary tower, I ached for you.
Tirelessly strived to prove my heart was true.
You'd find no time or warmth for me, no matter what I'd do.

I left you and you didnt understand it at the start.
I left to ease the pain of unrequited sting and smart.
I left you for the pain you poured on my cadaverous heart.
I left you, but the truth is; it was your choice to depart.

Art is for Everyone
Dave Brown

Writers writing, painters painting;
Critics hating the people taking
Art for themselves, to do as they please.
Art for art's sake, we express what we see.

Sculptors sculpting, singers singing;
Artists creating the passion they're feeling.
Written on paper or carved into stone:
The artists are gifted, though critics will moan.

Drummers drumming, builders building;
Not all will like the hidden meaning.
Enjoy these creations,don't crush them with hate.
Art is for everyone, not just for the Tate!

A Lover's Death
Sarah Tracy

In foetal position on concrete bed,
Like a scorned miscarriage, lying dead,
The abortion of one, love tried to bless,
The host was cold for the unwanted guest .

Abandoned to die a lover's death,
Remembrance of a last loving breath.
The silence takes over, the shadows move in,
The stillness - a madness to slowly begin.

Please rip out these eyes that lied to me
And tear out this heart that love couldn't see.
I beg you to cut this brain from my head,
I don't want to think - I'd rather be dead.

On this body please carve - deep in the bone,
The initial of one who turned it to stone.
For I want the world to know the name –
Indifference is the one to blame.

So Sad
Sarah Tracy

So sad - the withered rose, so red
Resembling the heart of one so dead.
Can it be healed? Will Love win through?
And let it blossom for us anew .

A Children's Story

Andrew Shiston

Alone and sleepy stood the Oak
Old brown and withered arms
Beside the brook and rickety barn
Forlorn and looking tired
Stood the old grey mare
And little pig with twenty little sire
Now awake and arms outstretched
And standing two foot higher
The old Oak shook his leaves
And in a shaky voice he said
'In all the years I've stood
My trunk has got much longer
But never have I drunk my fill
My roots are short of water'
The old grey mare and little pigs
And all the Oak trees friends
They dug a ditch across the field
And filled it full of water
Now the brook that trickled by the barn
That wound into the meadow
Flowed across the field and past the roots
And the old Oak tree drank his fill
From that day on the old grey mare
And all the Oak trees friends
Stood by the Oak in a leafy glade
Paid for by the water
Throughout the summer nights
And pleasant drowsy days
The old grey mare and all his friends
Walked in the trickling brook
And played around the meadow
Time went by and days were getting shorter
The old Oak tree was shedding leaves
And getting tired much quicker
The rickety barn by the trickling brook
Where the old grey mare and all his friends
Had grown up and used to wander
Had been repaired and all cleaned up
And now the nights were getting colder
The old grey mare and all his friends
Wandered back across the meadow
And walked back in the brand new barn

Where the nights would be much warmer
As winter came with jack frosts name
And the trickling brook froze over
The old Oak tree all by himself
Kept warm, by thinking come next year
The old grey mare and all his friends
Will come back across the meadow
As when the days are long and nights are short
It will be that much warmer

SHUT UP!

Andy Saunders

Cedric please leave me alone
As I settle down to write;
The sunset is so beautiful
And soon it will be night.

For three days now I've tried to write
And meditate so clear
But you have interrupted all
With continual squawking in my ear.

The sun is bout to lower itself
Onto horizons far away:
Oh, how stunning nature is
But you're getting in the way!
I won't be here tomorrow night
I'll be on the plane back home,
So please just let me write a poem
And watch the surf turn into foam.

SOME PARTIES ARE FUN
JOHN J. WHITMARSH

When I woke up one morning
As the sun was rubbing its eyes
And taking up his residence
In the palace of the skies,
I saw you there beside me
All innocent and pure
And wondered how I happened on
A woman so demure.

You found me at the party,
You said, as if that phrase
Would open up my memory,
Help me peer beyond the haze.
And you came back here, I started,
To share my bed with me?
I did, you said, now, if I may,
I'll share your history.

THE DEFLOWERING OF MISS PETAL

Carlton Hunt   (Performing floral sex)

Blossoming in ribbons and bows,
she's feeling thorny,
in any other game, a rose.

So quiet you could hear a snowdrop,
I nipped her in the bud,
Best in show, pick of the crop.

Searching for fools marigold
I kissed her on the tulips,
A pound a bunch, to have and to hold.

The scene of domestic violets,
With fertile thoughts in my head,
To plant her into my flowerbed.

Forget me not in the mass wisteria,
It was completely lupin,
Committing carnation sin

I'm totally head over heels in foxglove,
Absolutely blooming triffid, my son.

DENY EVERYTHING

STEVE TODD

"The Farting Rocks of Majuba Gorge,
A myth, scared us silly when we lay down to sleep.
We didn't expect such a dreadful noise-
It made our camels weep. All night,
Wet noises echoed round and round the crags,
Denying hours of rest before a solution was found.
A solution! Ultimate but, said Sarge, for the best.

We primed the dynamite, to the tune of toilet wrath:
The Farting Rocks squelched angry, ancient insults
that made us retch and breathe through khaki cloth.
No other way. I was at the back. The detonator was dodgy, so
we all watched with bated breath. As Briggs twisted it, the stuff
went up. With horror, we realised the danger.
A thousand years of methane tasted flame.
The flame agreed.
The fireball caught us all.

Iam the sole survivor of the (militarily denied)
Majuba Gorge Big Bang of '39.
They said 'A freak gas pocket. Tow the line!'
Know now- they lied."

NO CURE!

Paula Cleife

There aint no cure for being me,
What I have is a GIFT, not a disability!
You can KEEP your lithium and anti-d's
Cos there aint no cure for being ME!

I'm wild, I'm warm, I'm loved, I'm free.
The whole wide World's my friend, you see.
I can do the work of not one, but THREE
And there aint no cure for being ME!

I'll put your people on thir knees:
I'll squeal, I'll heal, I'll please, I'll tease;
Excite the minds of souls I squeeze.
There ain't no cure for being ME!

You wish you had my energy,
And HALF my personality.
You want to drug it out of me.
There aint NO CURE for being ME!

One day a computer will work
Scott Tyrrell

One day there'll be harmony.
There'll be tolerance and understanding and love.
One day there'll be peace and prosperity.
We'll fly on the wings of a dove.
One day a computer will work.
One day a computer will work.
One day a computer will work.
One day a comp...

OneOneOne

d............

Cntrl alt delete for the third time today,
And no, that didn't do any good.
I'll look in the window that lists the errors,
Ah, yes it's as clear as mud.

No, it's not having that at all.
I'll switch it off then switch it back on
If that fails, its going through the wall.
It's working! It's working! The indecipherable code
Is slowly filling my screen!
I know I didn't shut down properly last time!
I think I'm going to scream!

I'll open up Word, it's a simple enough task,
I'm sure it can manage that.
But no, the primary scratch disk is full,
Someone hand me a baseball bat!
I'll take a look in my C drive,
And see if there's anything I can bin.
Phtools? Wamsang? What the hell do these mean?
Someone fetch me a bottle of gin.

Right, Word's open, I'll finish this document,
But where the hell did the last paragraph go?
Of course, it crashed before I could save,
And all I can cry is NO!!!!!!!!!!
Yet another hour of my life is lost
To this merciless pile of crap.
If it tries anything else this evening,
I swear I'm going to snap.

Finally, this document's finished.
And I've been saving every five seconds.
All I have to do is print the thing out.
Glorious sanity beckons.
Page setup, portrait, HP laser jet 5,
OK, print. That's it!
What do you mean you can't find the printer?
It's sitting right beside you, you tit!

I'll check printer settings, they all look fine,
I'll check round the back of the machine.
Oh, the cable's stuck in the modem port,
I won't tell you what I say next, It's obscene!
One day a computer will work.
What a glorious day that will be.
Until then I'll go slowly berserk.
Until then I'll plead insanity.

Lonely Girl
Andrew Shiston

Forlorn and standing tall
In an empty dockyard basin
Bent and rusted rails
By broken fallen walls
Stood the lonely crane
Below her seized up wheels
And piles of mixed up cables
Lay her rusting tracks
That moved her back and forth
She'd suckled many ships
That docked along the pier
And lifted all the cargos
Until her day had come
No ships no men just rubbish
Drifting down the wharf

This Corrosion

Dragonslayer Tyu

The city lights with a million lights,
Burning the faces of inhabitants,
Toxic waste containers,
Used for fireplaces.

They sit alone, hidden, unnerved,
On the streets of the city,
No home, No family, No hope,
I can see the corrosion on their faces.

This is their December,
This may be their time of year,
This is their December,
Now it's all so clear,
I feel the pain,
And the Corrosion,
Brought to realisation,
In one primeval explosion,
The Government can't help us,
There's no one else that can,
We slipped into this void,
Paranoia is all we have left,
And it's altogether venomous,
Now it's going down,
Don't look into the mirror,
You'll see we are the clowns.
Sing this corrosion.

The Truth Is Out There

Thomas Moore

The universe is vast, they say,
and gravity is here to stay,
will man or nature pave the way?,
or is creative law just gay?
and are we impotent of mind?,
destined to seek but not to find
and is our future what's behind?
or is it just that we are blind?.

The question was not one of these,
nature would not, incline to please,
man is not given divine right
to understand from whence his might,
or even powers of second sight,
to forecast his eventual plight.
Rather his gift was that of reason
to plot the length of his own season
and if he does not heed to this,
it will be shorter than his wish.

Loveliness And Loneliness

Pete Nightingale

Two words, almost identical
To look at.
The whole world looks at loveliness;
Who looks at loneliness?

Invert the 'v'–
Loveliness
Becomes
Loneliness –
That easily.

Invert the 'n'–
Loneliness
Cannot be
Loveliness –
The whole world looks at loveliness;
No-one looks at loneliness.

Whispers in the Wind
Jeremiah Howard

Can you hear the harmonic sound,
Or feel the vibrations in the ground
Can you sense the thickness in the air,
Or is it that you do not care

With rays of sun hitting my feet
I hear the whispers, sounding discrete
They tell the secrets of the trees
As the wind places leaves upon my knees

The Earth quivers of pain and sorrow
Waiting on what God will bring her tomorrow
The whispers sound of angelic and sweet
As the earth crumbles beneath my feet

Under the moon and all the stars
I see the Earth and all her scars
With her dying breath she whispers in the wind,
"Heaven awaits you once again."

The Struggling Student
Ricky Kane

I'm gonna try some rhyme and rhythm,
It's what they want, so it's what I'll give 'em.
I'll even add some alliteration:
More literary morsels for mastication.

All this talk of iambic pentameter,
Only acts as a prisoner's perimeter,
They demand a simile to make it clearer:
Like the breaking of bars to bring the meaning nearer.

It's the writer's block they keep me in,
Away from the authors on the north wing,
Who can play with prose to print their feelings,
Whilst I'm trapped by techniques to create my meanings.

Still, shouldn't complain, now I've taken this stance,
And though my rhythm is hardly a dance,
Of getting a B, there's still a chance:
I've even used bloody assonance.

Ade Rowley

So, about me. I am 31 years old and live just outside Lincoln. I work full time as a VAT accountant and generally speaking, I absolutely hate the job! Yes, I am in the wrong job and yes, I do intend to get out as soon as I possibly can (although that will not be for some time yet). I am as gay as a tree full of parrots and live in my own tiny house, with my two cats (Broomstick and Tasha), alas, nobody wants to have sex with me (let alone live with me).

I have a rare disease called Brittle Asthma, which, for those of you who may be wondering, is the rarest and most lethal form of severe asthma (do not worry, it is not contagious). I write a lot of my own poetry, although precious few of them have ever been published, as they are not things which I share with the many, only the very few (somebody not a million miles from this page being one of them).

I think this is a really great and courageous venture for Paula to consider and I am proud to be a part of this. I hope that I am worthy of such a task as this and if my contributions help to bring anybody out of obscurity and into the light, then I am sure my life will have been worth something.

Ade's selection

The Turtle People
Miguel Angel Berrios

AMENDED BY ADE ROWLEY

The way to the village reminds me,
Of the time when I was born;
Naked, like any other human
At a time when innocence costs.
Little bodies crawling around me,
When I am not to behold,
I was taught that answers awaited,
Meanwhile we just chose to grow.
And leave behind a safer haven
That once was unknowledgeable days,
As we found the end of the crawling,
It was also the end of blind faith.
And there you stand, mother and father
With your hearts stampeding in race
When I grow, before you ever know
I will be what you never expected

Simple Things
Paula Cleife

I can look but I can't touch you
Like a diamond in a case
For you are hand-cut crystal
And I a clear glass vase.

You have your life in order
While mine's in disarray
For you are sculpted marble
And I hand-fashioned clay.

There's beauty in the simple things
I'm proud of what I am
For I am pure and honest
And you're a glitzy sham!

OLDSANDALS
BY MIGUEL ANGEL BERRIOS

WALKING THROUGH THE DESERT
NEVER HAS MEANT PROSPERITY
INDEED, IT HAS TAKEN AWAY
ALL THAT YOU CALL DIGNITY.

I USED TO TREASURE THESE OLD SANDALS
BUT NOW THEY ARE WORTH OF PAIN
IT SEEMS THE JOURNEY
FOR THEM WAS USELESS; VAIN.

BUT I FORGIVE GOD FOR HIS WISDOM
I FORGIVE HIM FOR HIS WAYS TO TEACH
MAYBE HE WILL FORGIVE ME TOO
FOR TURNING MY BACK ON HIM.

BESIDES, IT WAS MY NATURE
TO GROW OLD TO THIS LIFE
AND THEN AFTER ENDLESSLY TIRED,
RETURN TO DUST AND DIE.

I WEAR THEM BROWN AS OLD TREES
WHO WITNESS MY DEMISE
THIS OLD MAN WITHOUT WORDS
WAITING HERE IN LINE.

BUT I FORGIVE GOD FOR THE TESTING
I FORGIVE HIM FOR LETTING ME FAIL.
MAYBE HE IS JUST AS WELL, FORGIVING
AND I AM JUST TOO FRAIL.

One so young

Samantha Jones

Why are the young...taken so soon
When their lives have barely begun
Where do they go on their final journey
I believe that they follow the sun
To a better place where pain is no more
And beautiful gardens are found
Peace and love are the only emotions
And music the only sound
Be not afraid oh one so young
Pure magic is that you'll find
I may not be standing beside you
But I'll be just a whisper behind

Time to say Goodbye now

Alan Connor

Finally say so long,
Although our love was trying
We knew it wasn't wrong.

Time to dry my eyes now
To wipe away the tears,
Face the future on my own
Learn to live with all my fears,

So long my sweet sweet darling
It's finally come to a close,
I'm willing to let you go now
In words of simple prose,

I don't know how long it will shine
This burning beacon of my love,
But I know I must release you
Let you soar so high above,

I ask you to forgive me
For fighting you all the way,
All I ask is you remember me
At sometimes through your day,

And not think too unkindly
Of the lover you threw away,
I wish you well my sweet sweet love
For your happiness I will pray,

But remember the door is open
Twill open to the gentlest touch,
I suppose if guilty of anything
'Twas loving you too much.

.....I NEED
MIGUEL ANGEL

SOMEONE HAS GOT TO BE OUT THERE
AND KNOW THAT I, REALLY EXIST
SOMEONE MUST HAVE BEEN ON HIS KNEES TONIGHT
PRAYING HEAVEN SENDS SOMEONE LIKE ME.
I WILL BE THE ANSWER LONG AWAITED,
I WILL BE THE GREATEST SMILE UPON HIS FACE
GOD IS ALWAYS THERE, AS HE LISTENS TO YOUR PLEA
AND I AM HERE, SUDDENLY AWAITING ON HIS GRACE.

I NEED SOMEONE FAITHFUL AND SPECIAL,
SOMEONE THAT COULD ALWAYS READ MY MIND
KNOWING ME WILL BE AN EXPERIENCE, ETERNAL
SOMETHING IN THIS WORLD, SO HARD TO FIND.
I NEED A GROWN MAN IN THE FORM OF MIRACLE
WHO IS THERE STANDING STILL, AFTER ALL.
THAT EVEN WHEN HE HATES THE MUSIC I LOVE,
UNDERSTANDS ITS WORDS, DOES FILL MY HEART.

I KNOW TONIGHT, I FEEL I AM BREAKING
FOR GOD FORGIVES, BUT STILL I DO NOT UNDERSTAND
HIS UNWILLINGNESS ON ME, TO FIND THAT SOMEONE
WHEN HE KNOWS THAT IS ALL I REALLY WANT.
I CAN WAIT, BUT PATIENCE GROWS OLDER
AND IN THE MIRROR I AM NO LONGER WHAT I SEE
HEAVEN'S STILL A PLACE I LONG FOR,
BUT IT IS FAR FROM HERE ON EARTH...FROM WHAT I NEED.

LOVE'S EVOLUTION
Paula Cleife

I'll stand naked before you,
With you, I'm unashamed.
Kneel at your feet, adore you
But we are not the same.

A torturous lament will fill
This crazy, female brain.
To be unfilled and yet fulfilled
Because we're not the same.

I'll kiss your furrowed tension:
Incandescence is your name.
Revel in your attention
Although we're not the same.

Enjoy loves evolution
And our eternal flame:
Celebrate the resolution
That we are not the same.

Silent Limbo

Sarah Tracy

Trapped in a silent limbo, a land of loveless thought,
Meaning does not live there, these words can be bought.
Caught in a state of sorrow where 'Love'is hardly known,
A mere word for those who live there but never, ever shown.

A place where a lover's tenderness is rarely ever felt,
The hearts are made of stone there, they never, ever melt.
It's a land of unbelievers and people who can't trust,
The ones who feel no other's pain, their needs are a must.

Don't fall into this loveless land when bitterness calls your name,
You think you might be happy there? You need to call the blame?
This land is for the fallen few, the ones who cannot give,
Is this the place you're looking for? Is this where you will live?

Come open your heart and I'll show you a land, a place for us to go,
It's full of love and wonderful thoughts, it can help you heal and grow.
The land is right inside of you, open the door and lose the key,
The love you look so deeply for is here, right here, in me.

Come home my dear misguided love and find a restful view,
A place where you are welcomed and loved for being you.
Don't stray away when coldness comes and touches your sweet dream,
This love will keep the cold at bay and make your joy supreme

Dear God...

© *Scott Tyrrell May 2002*

I'm sorry about you and me.
I guess we just grew apart.
It felt like an arranged marriage, anyway-
Doomed from the start
Guess I never really knew you
And if you knew me, you never said
You were never there when it mattered
When I stumbled and when I bled
And what did you want from me?
We never really agreed.
Your contradictions only divided
The ones you chose to lead.

You promised so much if I followed you
And damnation if I did not
You demanded love by afflicting fear
I should have been off like a shot.
But it took some time to leave you
'Truth is you'd been around for so long
Knowing you was socially acceptable
You removed the need to be strong.
So please understand the strength it took
To crawl out from under your thumb
And know you'll always be part of me
I still say your name when I come.

But I bought out of your retirement plan
My life is no longer eternal
And you are no longer paternal
And death is no longer infernal
I don't need your crutch-promises anymore
And it's good to be finally free.
And if I fail or succeed
There'll be no one to blame but me.
Life is short, but life is big
And life is universal
It's rough, it's tough, it's potent stuff
And life is not a rehearsal.
I'm sorry I won't be climbing
Your Shangri-La-rian tree
But I never needed you
And you never needed me.

Through these eyes

Amy Baldry

I lay on a bed of roses and thorns
I lay and watch the figure that mourns
I lay on a bed of towering fears
I lay and watch it dry it's tears

I see what others seem to not
I see the dreams it has forgot
I see what stirs it's deep soul
I see the pain caused by an empty hole

I stand in the shadows to see its dark night
I stand and watch the stars of light
I stand in deep thoughts of my life
I stand and watch it in all it's strife

I fly and hover above it's head
I fly and see it's heart is dead
I fly and hover, try to mend whats broke
I fly and see it cough and choke

I watch the angels dancing free
I watch it watching me
I watch the fairies in the trees
Talking to the passionate breeze

I dream I feel the leopard's stare
I dream I feel the wind blow through my hair
I dream I feel the rains embrace
I dream I feel the power in the panthers chase

I feel it breath in and out
Doubting what lifes all about
I feel it's soul, intense and tight
I feel it yearning to take flight

I will watch from where I lay
I will watch and here I stay
I will float in space surrounded by it's words
On the back of white winged birds.

MEANINGFUL

MIGUEL ANGEL

In, walks the tempest unaware
That the lives it claims, do belong
To unfortunate hearts beating their names
From the earth on inertia, down below.

When the night ends without the conquest
Of those who possess the stronger one.
Who will know the hour when trumpets?
Announce an alternate ending's begun.

And life which was meaningful, always
Will fade with the tide's softer side.
We will never be empty of emotions
But why do you need them, tonight?

When things are everything but needful,
When your heart is an echo in the dark.
Do I expect the ancient of memory?
Carry on, the mourning that far.

In my arms there was always a space
Awaiting to welcome you in,
But there was never the available time
Where I actually would have seen.

That love is not always the kindest
When you talk to the demons inside
Here I am, bleeding in silence
Veins regretting, the cold of the knife.

Dave Seaman

Dave Seaman (that's me!) is an author and poet currently living in London,
England. He has self-published two books, a poetry collection ("Warts &
All") and a comedy sci-fi series ("The Captain Disaster Collection Volume
I"). After quite a long break, I have started writing poetry once more, due
to the inspiration that has come from the new (and permanent!) love of my
life, Rebecca. (It's all sickeningly happy now! ;-O)
In fact it's almost all as slushy as this one that I've just written:

Just Can't Say Goodbye

I never want to say goodbye,
If that happened I'd surely die.
I cannot tear myself away,
Not tomorrow, and not today.
My love for you is great, you see;
I know you feel the same for me.
My love for you will never end;
On that, my love, you can depend/
I'll never ever go away,
As long as you want me to stay.
Because, no matter how I try,
I can't manage to say goodbye!

Fortunately (??), there was a time when I was rather less ecstatically happy
all the time, and I wrote rather more morbid poetry, such as:

Life and Death

The raindrop slides slowly
down the windscreen,
like a teardrop falling
down a cheek.
Reaching the bottom,
it is engulfed
and disappears from sight,
swept aside by
merciless wiper blades,
cut off in the prime
of its journey.
The rain continues falling,
yet never can any individual raindrop
be replaced
Another tear appears,
joining the torrent.

Dave's selection

Love Dies

Christopher Michael Palmer

A love found,
A love lost,
Tears of joy,
Tears of pain.

We were so good,
It turned out so bad,
You lifted my soul,
You tore up my heart.

We smiled all the time,
We fought all the while,
I loved you for you,
You turned me away.

I wanted too love you,
I tried all the time,

My efforts were wasted,
For now you're not mine.

DAMAGE, INC.

Miguel Angel

Little girl collect those flowers
precious in your little dress
tell Mama you didn't know then
how the green grass felt.
But now you know
and sadly you regret,
that uncle Tom's dirty hands
were really damage games.
Taste the madness in your eyes
where purity is gone,
and in exchange, here's your reward,
the crown that Jesus wore.

The Face of Death
Sarah Tracy

The face of death is stark and staring
It always looks upon sorrow and guilt
It is cold and unfeeling
It never smiles, not winks its eye
Its mouth gapes open in a silent scream
Its last words forever echo
Its fear is imprinted upon it
It never looks upon love again

SUICIDE MUSIC
Miguel Angel

A piano solo,
through the halls of isolation,
it makes sense the rush of blood
the surge of pure transgressions.
The notes in symphony
crescendos in the urge,
the life that fills the violin
slowly fades in turn.
It takes your life away
without a trace of pain
and when you lie awake,
without a breath,
the music starts again.

Lost Love
Geoff Hough 2002

Lost love - would that it vanished complete from the heart,
Vanquished and cleansed to restart fresh anew.
Though fathoms of longing, yearning, linger,
And cobwebs spun on that once thought eternal and true.
Preserved, petrified they remain to scar loves yet to be,
To tarnish and dim new found hope and faith;
The past casting long shadows over future bright fields.

SNOW WHITE HOMICIDE

STEVE TODD

Weapon: Bad Apple
Obviously
Time of Sleeping Death:
Around half past three.

You'd credit those dwarves
with a little more sense
than a hungry Princess
for home defence.

(During the questioning
all became clear;
the 'Housekeeper'deal
had been Dopey's idea.)

The autopsy findings
were no great surprise,
Just that forceps OR kisses
could open her eyes.

Granny Smith's prints
were all over the place!
Send the FBI home;
It's an open/shut case.

The Train

Francis Smith

You fold your knees
and I hear the soft swish of silken thighs
It's no surprise my thoughts persuade my eyes
to follow the curvy contours of your breast
and then continue on their journey
to explore the rest.
Your legs unfold and I see a glimpse of
sparkling white, so bright.
You smile and fill the empty space and I in fantasy
caress each curve across your face.
We tremble in dreamy pleasure as we rise
together stumbling from the train.
Then we embrace 'til darkness
falls and banishes the rain.

"We Three Are One"
STEVE TODD

I dwell in the thickest of summer thorns
And when the wind roars and rages, and doth break
To and fro, from the ridges to the soaring things
Iam the force that withers the sedge from the lake.
When culture lived in Mansion Rooms
and well-stuffed aristocrats trod the boards,
Their slave-things called me 'Blight',
Unknowing I had lived before-
My years mapped out in epithets of doom

For when night falls, my will be done- in blood.
They do their parlour tricks to pass the time
'Til I can judge, and cast debauchery down
and give them mercy-sleep in mud and slime.
I leave them pure, I leave their bodies pale
I steal and sculpt their breath from Hill to Dale
And when their friends depart, and earthworms drool,
I add the gravestone etching 'One More Fool'.

Step once, but soft; these are hard times
These movements shape your final dance.
'The Knight, The Maiden- One Romance'
It's written- these dreams dull like wine.
For wisdom, wounded, finds a home
in the ignored, the Old and Broken;
Beat and spat on to the last, and
Clinging to the crumpled token.

Gentle Was The World
John J Whitmarsh

Gentle was the world with its warming sun,
And soft was the mood of the new-mown field;
Tender was my humour as I looked ahead
To the promise of the season and the bright, wide sky.

Placid was the day when the last tired star
Departed from the sky with a winked adieu;
And gentle was the air when the scented breeze

Stirred meadow grasses where the horses grazed.
Mild was the light around breakfast time,
When skylarks tumbled from their heather beds
To snap floating insects from the pleasant air,
And serene was the mood of the world at large.

Gentle was the water in the shallow brook
As it washed away sleep of the night just gone,
And peaceful was the sound of the bees' quiet hum
Beyond the tranquil silence of the market town.

And gentle were our steps as my love and I
Took to the trail with our whispered plans;
And gentle was the route that conveyed us up
To the tattered heathland where shy rabbits hid.

Slow were the clouds as they stepped in tune
To the breath of the zephyr with no urgency;
And cool were the shadows as they strolled across
The sheep-peopled uplands where time stood still.

Gentle were your eyes as they looked to mine
And asked me questions with an eloquent glint;
Soft was my answer when I spoke my love,
And enchanting was our world on that magic moor.

Silent was the town when we at last returned,
And empty were the streets with the market done;
Content were we now we had made our bond
And blissful were we then in that gentle world.

TXT
© Scott Tyrrell 2001

HI M8
RUOK?
SORY TO CALL SO L8
BUT I JST BORT A FONE 2DAY
+ I JST CDNT W8
2 TEL EVRY1 I EVA MET
ABT MY NU FOUND JOY
NOW I CAN TLK IN GIBRISH
2 EVRY GRL + BOY!

BUT IT DNT STOP THER!
O NO
I CAN TLK IN PCTRS 2!
I CAN BE :-)
:-(
:-D
:-O
I CAN GIV U A BIG :-* 2!

I CAN B :-II
%-)
:-P
I CAN ;-)
+ NOT ONLY THAT
I CAN :'-(
I CAN :-@
I CAN B A *:-)
I CAN TEL U I'M d:-)

THN ALL I DO IS CLK SND
I CAN CNTCT U EVEN IN BED
BUT I JST RUN OUTA CREDT
SO I'LL RNG U 2MORO INSTD.

:-)	happy
:-(	sad
:-D	laughing
:-O	surprised
:-*	kiss
:-II	angry
%-)	confused
:-P	tongue-in-cheek
;-)	wink
:'-(	cry
:-@	scream
*:-)	clown
d:-)	wearing a hat

Dark and Gray

Jeremiah Howard

The night was lonely and gray,
With shadows dancing all the day.

A single silhouette approaches me.

And with a flicker of light,
He disappears into the night.

A silver rose lay on the ground,
Where he vanished from sight and sound.

Another silhouette approaches me.

This time he starts to weep,
Turns and begins to creep.

And with a flicker of light,
He disappears into the night.

A silver rose lay on the ground,
Where he vanished from sight and sound.

A shorter silhouette approaches me.

This one with long, curly hair,
A silver rose is what she bears.

She turns to walk away,
Only to hear me say,

"What is this? Where am I?"
"You know you didn't have to die!"

She replied with a soft tone.
My heart throbbed as I began to moan.

And with a flicker of light,
She disappeared into the night.

A gray rose lay on the on the ground,
Where she vanished from sight and sound.

Tempt Me At Forty
John J Whitmarsh

Will you tempt me at forty
To wild new adventures,
To try and to do things
That I've only dreamed of?

Will you help me sail skywards,
Heart-free and daring;
Will you gently persuade me
To kill age-rooted habits?

Will you help me break out,
And become shallow, not mellow;
Will you help me deserve
What my betters achieve?

Will you give me the kick
To break out of my orbit;
Will you give me the push
To leap from the cliff?

Will you tempt me at forty
To wild new adventures,
Or will I scowl at you always
For holding me back?

How Do I Say It's Over
Lois Engle

I loved you when I first met you, It all happened so fast,
I held on so tight, though I knew it wouldn't last.
My feelings grew stronger as time had gone by,
Never did I realize you'd be the one to make me cry.
I stood by your side even when I didn't agree,
Moving into the shadows when you'd humiliate me.
I trusted you -- oh yes -- like no one ever before,
Only to realize you'd hurt me once more.
I've tried to express the feelings that I hold now,
With fighting so much, you say, "hold on," but how?
I guess what I'm saying is my heart growing colder,
As I search for the words to tell you, "It's over!"

'Til Death Do Us Part

Shannon Diaz

She came bearing flowers, she was in love, this girl who never had a doubt
Until a terrifying September day never expected or thought about
She was on her way to meet her love, the one who filled her soul
Arriving at the silent scene would be her fate that is being told

Time seemed to race around her as she waited patiently at the Cafe
And she walked to the door to view the Manhattan sidewalk repeatedly that day
Feeling strangely anxious, still waiting, she reached for a tissue to catch her tear
Because for five long years, for coffee every day, they agreed to meet right here

Fear raced through her body as she heard the most terrible thing
A noise so horribly indescribable she was convinced this was all a dream
Was it an explosion? A crash of some kind? What horror could this be?
A flash of sobriety rushed her mind as she remembered her beloved Pete

Far off in the distance chaos and running footsteps could be heard
Someone yelled, "Its on fire, its on fire" she raced to the door to be re-assured
Her face then had a look of despair as she took the doorway by the hand
She knowingly realized god had taken the life of an irreplaceable man

The girl had thought at first that maybe Pete was still on his way
Perhaps he wasn't in his office on the 96th floor that day
She instantly bowed her head and placed her hands together to pray
For the obvious death of so many people and her heart breaking great dismay

Another plane approached a building, fear and adrenaline through her brain
She looked up at agony to the two towers that were her lover's last stop off the train
The girl ran down the crowded panicked streets screaming out his name
With steady flowing tears down her cheek, never to be the same

Sometimes she still comes to meet him with flowers in her hand
Except the meeting place has changed in which now god is in command
She now must meet a cemetery and a stone that bears his name
Until their spirits are reunited in heaven, she'll remain saddened and in pain

Angels reside in heaven and keep her heart content on the fact
That Pete is not gone forever, and she will meet him with their love intact
The Souls from September who lost their lives will always be able to sing
They just have lost their flesh and blood but gained a set of wings

Who me?

© *Scott Tyrrell 2001*

All you people
You don't know me.
You don't know one line
Of my biography
You don't know where I'm from
You don't know if you care
But opinions are forming
As you continue to stare.

As your brains scan the stereotypes
To see which box I belong.
You're becoming intrigued
Cos its taking too long.
Can you see me yet?
Can you see through?
Tell you what
I'll give you a clue.

I want to be happy.
I'm often sad
I'm jealous, I'm sullen
I'm grateful, I'm glad.
I've failed and succeeded
I've been blessed and betrayed
I've rejoiced and regretted
The choices I've made.

I've kicked a cat,
I've hugged a tree
I've been a fascist
And a hippy.
I've fought for peace
I've come to blows
I've stepped back for others
I've stepped on toes.

I've demanded privacy
I've craved attention
I've lied more times
Than I can mention.
I seek truth
In all its guises
I often hide
When it arises.

My love could build a thousand
bridges
My rage could split the atom
Some days I don't get out of bed
Some days I'm up and at 'em
I've been lost and found
And fixed and broken.
I've scoffed the words
That I have spoken.

I've squandered the gifts
I've been afforded.
I've been abused
I've been applauded.
I've been an altruist, a capitalist
A communist and a bum.
I've called for silence
I've banged the drum.

I've prayed for rain
I've worshipped the sun
I've stood and fought
I've turned and run
I am good, I am bad
And everything inbetween.
Just like you.
Just a human being.

If you Fall
Shannon Diaz

If teardrops fall and the sky turns grey
I will pick you up and take you away
I will hug you and make you feel loved so much
Caress you with my sympathetic touch

If raindrops fall and your eyes drop down
I will be there to take away your frown
I will express to you the sweetest things
Let you into my sacred dreams

If the horizon is darkened and the day is damp
I will send you a letter with a cheerful stamp
I will show you my heart deep inside
We'll talk to each other with nothing to hide

If thunder growls and birds don't sing
Love and beauty my heart will bring
I'll present to you the best gift yet
And that is for you to feel no regret

If things look hard and seem never to end
I'll give you two of my hands to lend
I will look into your eyes and be your light
I will embrace your soul and keep it held tight

FIRE BY NATURE
Jörgen Jansson

They've been nearby too many years
Brothers by hot blood and frozen tears
They walked before me, my guardians
They told me to act on every chance

I've been beyond eternity to reach my confidant of core
A flower with soul, needed to find what I was looking for
I reached high over them heights, seeking for a better one
Now I have found love's delights, the lonely days are gone

She's been waiting for so long
Within all the lines in her song
She's the girl behind the centrefold
My long lost gal, the one spirit told

So I lit the fire by nature, have it all so lets boogie and roll
Still got the hot blood and I'm not missing the frozen tears
Yeah! She's the fire of nature, one glance and I had to roll
Still live in dynamic faultless vision without threats & fears

Me I don't know right from wrong
Me I used to hear her in every song
So it still goes on, It's the same refrain
So good in heart, she's all I can sustain

Been beyond beliefs, she will soon walk in trough my door
My flower within soul, don't need to be without any more
I reached high over them heights, seeking for the only one
Now I have found love's delights, the lonely days are gone

This is my love, Ill do anything to amuse
My wanted wild one, my persevering fuse
It's my adorable black rose flame
The one I want in a heated game

So I lit the fire by nature, have it all so lets boogie and roll
Still got the hot blood and I'm not missing the frozen tears
Yeah! She's the fire of nature, one glance and I had to roll
Still live in dynamic faultless vision without threats & fears

I've seen the eyes that gleams many times in the sky
Miss Bluesheart slide back in to my side, I tell you why
I light the fire by nature, got to keep my eyes open wide
I light the fire by nature, got to leave brotherhood aside

What Do I Say?

Rebecca Smith

What do I say today to my love,
The one who inspired me,
So many poems to write.
Who inspired me too,
To say the words, (joyous words)
Which changed my life forever.

When you came into my life,
I had no idea of how,
My life would blossom.
Or that you would forever be,
My one and only true love,
And give me joy forever.

So what do I say to you now,
But, that I love you,
Need you, want you and
Oh so completely adore you!

This Empty House

Shannon Diaz

I looked around the house and you weren't there
I walked to the kitchen table and pulled up a chair
I waited a while longer and then I began to sigh
I can never stop thinking about you and I

I put the chair back in its place at the table
I tried to sit down, but found I'm not able
I walk to the radio and push the power on
I listen to the words of a tender love song

I evolve into hysteria as I try and be calm
As I listen to the words of this powerful song
I hear the lyrics as if they were written for me
About two lovers in pain who chose to flee

I relive our glorious days when we shared
I take out old letters that prove that we cared
I look at this empty house and get frozen with fear
So scared that this emptiness will persist around here

Lively Lil
Samantha Jones

Sitting on the bench at night, watching passers by
Some of them would make her laugh, others make her cry
Watching as they hurried home, exhausted by the day
Some were happy, others sad as they passed by her way
Longing to confide in them but they would never know
The loneliness she felt and the fear she could not show
They knew her just a 'Lively Lil'a joke for all to share
How could she let them know she wanted somebody to care
Sighing sadly to herself as the moon descended low
Curled up tightly on the bench...for she had nowhere else to go

Where to Now
Derek Batchelor

When the sound of a voice just reflects of formality
then accept that the feelings have died,
Pick yourself up get your mind back in order
after all for so long you had tried.
Yes its nice when in love and the feelings run high
if you`re paired right it could last forever,
The fact so remains that one cannot please all
irrispective how hard one's endeavour.

Once relationship sours the one wishing to leave
has already made plans to effect,
The longer the leaving of the one asked to go
will earn quickly just more disrespect.
But then such is life more so now than ever
the days of long marriage seem gone,
What you had was so nice but its not coming back
so stop kicking yourself and move on.

The Secret From My Past

Lois Engle

I think I found a vision, I think I finally see the light,
It happened sitting late last night, my mind had gone to flight.
I saw you standing by me, your face was showing shame,
A tear had fallen from your face as you chanted my name.
Your eyes were trying to express the words you couldn't say,
Confused I was for I didn't know, what would make you react this way.
I tried everything to comfort you, in hopes to understand,
Just as I thought I'd never know, you reached out for my hand.
Looking deep into your eyes my soul started to ache,
To stop myself from crying out, deep breaths I had to take.
You asked me if I loved you, enough to understand,
Something that happened in the past, something that wasn't planned.
My mind was racing trying to think what could have been so bad,
Memories of love when I was young was all I've ever had.
You stated you were sorry, for ruining my life,
You knew I was your child, I could never be your wife.
You begged for my forgiveness, for erasing from my mind,
The disgusting things you did to me when I was only nine.
Now I understand more of the life I seem to live,
I'm never getting anything, I always have to give.
My emotions are never balanced, my head seems to always ache,
Happiness is so hard to find, and real love, it seems too fake.
But now that you have let me know a bit about my life,
It's easier to understand why my life's been full of strife.
Now I can get some honest help, to heal my heart at last,
Now that I know and can accept the secret from my past.

The Loss of My Heart!
Christopher Michael Palmer

Trapped in loneliness,
My heart cries out in silence,
My hands reach out to hold you,
But you no longer are there.

I cry myself to sleep again,
For the Twelfth Night of never,
I feel the darkness surround me,
I feel it choking my heart.

I cry out from my broken sleep,
I chant your name again,
The loneliness surrounds me,
Squeezing the life from my heart.

I drift off into silence,
The storm building from within,
I try to reason with my fear,
But the silence beats my screams.

So many nights you have been my rock,
So many times conquering my fear,
No more do I feel your love,
My heart just disappeared.

Sarah Tracy

Paula said, "Write what you want." So here goes. To be or not to be....in this book....is a sheer joy for all of us :o)
"I'm not a poet!" I once said to Paula and she sweetly replied, "Shut up and send some more poems." I love her for that - she is an inspiration and a true friend.
My life is simple; it can be defined by the people who love me. My sons, John and Joe, who make me giggle and keep my soul filled with pure joy, even when it is sulking! My mother, who still gets excited for me, even when it is only because I didn't burn the egg. My Love, who I missed before I even met him and who makes dreams and wishes come true. And my new friends: sensitive poets, lovers of life that fill me with a sense of wonder and constantly renew my faith in humanity with their words. My life is the richest in the world because of these bright gems that graced my path.
I am the 42 year old, (honest) Irish poet (yes Paula, I said, a poet!) and the library assistant that the readers shush.
I am honoured to be a part of this.

Timeless Heroes

Collage of thought, memories long
Inspire to paint the moments gone
When men were heroes on a page
And women never seemed to age

A time when love, a hidden view
could still be found safe and true
Not splashed with ugly read and green
Predator Aids on the scene

When mothers still needed a father's hand
To etch the life of their little man
And landscapes rose to painter's need
Now gaping sores of toxic greed

Oh! Where is the air, so sweet in scent
That poets drank and heaven sent
The words they wrote for times to come
When memories fade and beauty's done

Now, the writers are rebels and the poets scream
For the moment has gone to be calm and serene
In the blazing sun, my tears turn to salt
For the beauty we lost from this once treasure vault

But I'll still read the pages, though they be scorched
And gaze at the landscapes that haven't been torched
Collage of thought, memories long
Inspire to paint? The moment's gone

Sarah's selection

WHEN I AM A WOMAN
Miguel Angel

Roses, they mean I am just like them
Beautiful, fragile and just then,
Overwhelming to human sight
When I am woman in the rain.

I wear thorns, like a pearl necklace
Remember?, the gift of the first.
It is sad, after so many anniversaries
The weight is a cross I can't bear.

When I am a woman, I am
What you are never, able to achieve.
From multiple, extravagant orgasms
To finding the silence when I bleed.

When I am a woman I'm stronger
Than the muscles in your arms,
Because I use mine to embrace you
Not to cause you any harm.

So beat me tonight, it is raining
No one will save me from you.
Maybe, and after all I am weaker,
And men are those chains we can't loose.

Another Day
Sarah Tracy
(in reply to the above poem by Miguel Angel Berrios)

Weep not for me as I bleed
For I will rise and reap the healing ray.
Weep for the one who shed my blood
For he will sink to don another day.
And there he'll bleed and understand
The pain I once knew.

THE MUSKETEER

Jörgen Jansson

In the depth of my soul there's a river of tears
Hey you Philomel! Words are flouting in my mind
I wish you could write us another song
I wish I could have done anything for you

Oh Lord, I've been waiting for the right octave
Oh my God, I really been trying to write it
Oh Lord, how I want to hear that perfect ode
Oh please my God, won't you help me to find it

I like to give the rocker what I can
This dedication is for the special man
To the man with a thousand lyrics
To the musketeer of rock & roll

You man from Emerald Isle, you still live within us
Irish man in heaven above, you still play for us
A musketeer with fighting words, a basic musketeer with glow
In my book of great poetry you're on every page

At night I can see the wild one walking the Elysian fields
The musketeer is playing the harp for another king
He will not ever stop bringing back good old memories
The musketeer he's not alone doing the wild thing

I read them good old lyrics and in the wind I hear the angels whistle
So well the sentences are put together, the harmony takes me high
In north and south the musketeer is the icon on the wall
In east and west a rock`n'roll hero never fades at all

Oh Lord, I remember the early days of admiration
Oh my God, I long for them notes we never heard
Oh Lord, I wonder where you would be right now
Oh my God, the rose I bought is still bleeding for you

I would like to give you what I can
This proclamation is for you my man
To you, the man with a rock & roll attitude
You disappeared and left a trace to follow

You man from Emerald Isle, you still live within us
Irish man in heaven above, you still play for us
A musketeer with fighting words, a basic musketeer with glow
In my book of great poetry you're on every page

At night I can see the wild one walking the Elysian fields
The musketeer is playing the harp for another king
He will not ever stop bringing back good old memories
The musketeer he's not alone doing the wild thing

Mother of God, what more can I say?
God gives us endless care and devotion
Messiah lives with the one we all love
We all live this life then we follow him
Right on up, away to his kingdom come

That Special Place

Dave Seaman

There is a seat in this canteen
where inspiration flows through me
and I write lucid, beautiful poetry
and prose.
Unfortunately
someone else is sitting in it.

The Spider
Mike Helps 2002

The spider spins her world
Amongst the dust and bones
Of all the love she'd ever known.
Little mother.

She is sin,
Soft black velvet, eyes in the dark
Blood on her teeth, marks on my skin.

She spreads her lies,
Like her legs,
All around her, love and disease
And begs "Is this Poison?
Or everything you need?"
One taste will tell.

I offer myself.

I'm bound,
Twisted and breathed right in.
Barely breathless I'm wrapped
Deep down inside her
Dark darkness
Deadly, warm and harmless.
Smother me and cry yourself to sleep.

To Conquer The Physical
Geoff Hough

Waves of love across oceans deep,
Crests of hope riding high and free.
Physical divides be they vast or steep
Cannot conquer what's meant to be.
Fate may be cruel,
Sometimes kind,
Often fey,
Even blind.
But if we're sure footed,
Built to last,
Nothing can stop what will come to pass.

Black Widow or Pussycat?

John J Whitmarsh

She spoke
(Without words)
With her shining eyes,
And used her expression
To hypnotise
Her watching
And eagerly waiting
Prey,
And looked
At him
As if to say:
'Come hither, my love,
Come give me your all,
Come fall to the spell
Of my bright eyes'thrall.'
And he read
And deciphered
The unspoken prose,
And replied
With a look
And a tilt of his head –
Then she moved
Ever slowly
As he waited in dread
For the pounce,
For the stab
Of her predatory claws –
But sighed in relief
When she purred
'I am yours!'

THE EQUAL INSIDE
Paul White

the equal inside of me
stains like a rash
when it tries to break free.

when wondering how
all became such as this
the equal inside of me
stands to the side of me
watching and waiting
intending on being me

the equal inside of me
often surrounding me
pulling and tugging and trying
to conquer me

deep deep deep breaths
enforcing harsh clarity
the equal inside is not me

a misnomer for sure
unequal in parity
(temporarily) silent once more

the equal inside of me
the wolf at the door

Shooting star
Samantha Jones

I'll search beyond the sky at night to find a shooting star
No-one will know our secret, but I'll know who you are
This star will have a special name, belonging just to you
And when I dream my dreams alone...I'll save one dream for you

WILD PERFECTION
Dave Brown

YOUR BEAUTY
Not the classic paleness of a cold, Winter morn
More the richness and warmth of an early Autumn day
As the sunlight pierces throught golden strands
Lighting up your face, your beaming smile
The finishing touch, brings overflowing emotion, your inner beauty.

YOUR LOVE
So strong for those who share with you their life
trusting you with their heart, they know will be in good hands
Friend or lover, adult or child, you give love unconditionally
All or nothing the only way you know.
Your unbridled passion, the very essence of your love.

YOUR SOUL
So impulsive, you lead blindly for fun and frivolity
Throwing caution to the wind, your laughter and smile
Lighting up others lives and your passion exploding in all you do
Then you feel yourself falling, uncontrollable, frightening, dark.
You must hold on tight to retain your soul.

I Miss You Like.....
Paula Cleife

Hai Karate and Old Spice,
Shake 'n'vac housewives
And those furry dice;
Songs of Praise on a Sunday,
Wombles, Dr. Who:
All these things I hated!
See: I don't miss you!

BUT

As for my friends:
Well, they're shaker makers;
All that I wanted but never deserved!
Angel Delight, Delia,
Rolf's Stylophones;
Inflatable furniture,
Beatles and Stones.

ON A SEA OF DEVOTION

Jörgen Jansson

Perception gives me courage to wait
In all shadows I have found a reason
I know I feel consent easier right now
Teasing feelings makes yearning worth while

I've learned to embrace possibilities
That ability moves towards passion
All well known senses within us all
I will give, I will share with you love

On a sea of devotion thoughts drift away
You heat up my life to the limit, my flame
On a sea of devotion I won't lose anything
Share my heart cause you've read my soul
On a sea of devotion love grows into my mind
On a sea of devotion I dream of one of a kind

Delight is winding a ball in my mind
Don't need more expert knowledge
Love is the conception purling in me
Fulfilled of the thirst I need no advise

You still wonder what's inside my silence
Need it be discerned more honestly?
I will give you all the necessary answers
Can you spare me all the love in heart?

On a sea of devotion thoughts drift away
You heat up my life to the limit, my flame
On a sea of devotion I won't lose anything
Share my heart cause you've read my soul
On a sea of devotion love grows into my mind
On a sea of devotion I dream of one of a kind

Never will I steal what you have in soul
I wanna share delight, have a richer life
To delude you is to deny my better self
I like to give my life to a beautiful world

Maybe I wish for more than I have earned
I believe there's a bridge to all pleasantness
You ought to now know where to find light
It doesn't take a letter to give you that kiss

From a sea of devotion I'm moving in closer
From a sea of devotion you will see me walking
Without a sea of devotion there could be no dream
Without a sea of devotion you never knew I was the one

Decisions
Sue Whitmarsh

He stands at the crossroads:
Roads fan out,
Their destinations hidden by horizons.

There are signposts
Dimly marked –
Which way to go?

The first holds the promise of ultimate success,
But it toils uphill,
Unrelenting and steep;

The second, an easier downhill slope,
With pathways at either side.
Which will he choose?

I stand and watch,
Hoping and fearing, as
He stands at the crossroads.

SHE AND HE
Peter Nightingale

For a man
To have his head buried
In the long,
Draped hair
Of a woman

Is to return:
To return

To the mists of his childhood,
To the warmth
And the incense
That should ever be his.

Does woman,
In giving him this,
Relate to old memories

Of stubble and smoke,
To a malodorous
Maleness

Destined always
To be a dry rasp
On the skin of her life?

The World Was A Summer Of Electric Midnights
Andrew Penland

the world was a summer of electric midnights,
like the seconds before Cinderella's last dance:
sunsets painted with orange juice and blood
surrendered the sky to liquid green stars.
children wrote hymns and chased fireflies;
chime-notes rained from the clouds like tears.
lion clubs and rocketships flirted with each other,
shy eyes innocence and free as jazz.
fantasy and future coalesced into kisses
shared (though not tasted) over abstract space.
Romeo hadn't met Juliet yet but Jesse James had hung
up his guns and retired--that's when these
nocturnes were lovingly thought, half-memories,
half-dreams, of a lonely lost time.

The Crusade of My
Gareth Smith

I wandered as a whisper,
A shadow and a spirit.
I promised not to call her,
To follow or to visit.
I set about my breaking,
My crusade and my story.
I remade myself for her,
For my heart, for my glory.

I returned as an earthquake,
A full moon and a livewire.
I forced my heart upon her,
My memories, my desire.
I confessed my forced rebirth,
My voyage and my vision.
Oh, how the sweet light had dimmed;
How misguided this mission.

FLASHBACK
Dave Brown

EYES OPEN; QUICKLY SHUT.
HEAD POUNDING, BACK THROBBING.
OPENING EYES SLOWLY THIS TIME.
BED FEELS HARD AND DAMP.

EVERYTHING ON IT'S SIDE?
MATTRESS FEELS LIKE.........AHH CARPET
SOGGY AND WINESTAINED
NOTHING FAMILIAR; TRY TO GET UP.

INCREASING HEAD PAIN; TRY TO FOCUS
AS OBJECTS ROTATE NINETY DEGREES.
NOT MY HOME.......SMALL FLASHBACK.....
LAST NIGHT.........OH MY GOD!!!!

THE WHORE
Andrew Penland

the whore
lays down in a cathedral door
sculpting a rose from a rubber hose
watching the sky
for UFOs
and police.
it seems the rain will never cease
and the night is all tension
without release.
lost in dream,
herself sighs
like the broken crystal
of an angel's eyes
the silence is ripped by
a baby's cries
as the sun slowly sweeps
the darkness away.

The Storm

Andrew Shiston

Far out beneath the boiling clouds
Where sea and sky thus meet
A savage storm with lightning bolts
Meet the waters summer heat
They join and intertwine
A union of might and strength
Far out at sea and not near land
They mate and twist and turn
Until their inner force of winds
Decides their place to go
The inner vortex of this storm
That reaches to the sea
Sucks everything within its reach
To fill the hungry need
Within its darkest deepest place
That feeds upon this greed
A shaft of gleaming light appears
That lights the twisted face
The winds abate blue sky above
Far out at sea beneath the clouds
The storm has lost its way....

After a night shift
John J Whitmarsh

When the wind is colder than a harridan's stare
And frost sits on branches like white tipped knives,
And when the clouds black out the bright moon's face
And the bus is late and the birds still sleep,
Think back to the factory with its hot air blowers
And its loud lullaby of machines at work
And its endless tea and its endless chat
And the endless hours to the finishing bell,

Or look forward to the bed where she left her mark
When she rolled out softy at the clock's first cry,
And think then of the kiss, of the half-asleep smile,
Of the panic as she leaves with her lipstick smudged.
When the wind is colder than a harridan's scowl
And the night was long and the dawn is harsh
Think on to the bed that awaits your head
And forget the factory and the sleeping birds.

Dream
Mike Helps 2001

Last night, I dreamt of you.
We were just walking
Through the streets we knew.
Hand in hand,
With that special grip,
The only one that seemed to fit.

Pete Bishop

Was a panelist for a short while and we are most grateful for his contribution ☺
Pete has also supplied our very first cover image.

Coming up for Air

We act like we are invincible
Have we not learned anything?
Of the great battles of history
Of the mortality of men?

We pretend that things will always last
When we know that they will fade
That relationships will stay the same
As the day that they were made

We pontificate about the way a
Person should behave
In situation from birth up to the grave

Well I'm coming up for air now
I'm pushing fear aside
I'm thinking life anew now
Which values to abide

I know I won't be always right
But my mistakes will be my own
Instead of those imposed by
State and Church and Throne

Pete Nightingale

Having known Paula Cleife for about three or more years in cyberspace - and having been on the receiving end of her very empathetic e-mails when I was going through something of a personal crisis (thank you, Paula, in public) - I nevertheless missed her opening weeks at the Peoples'Poet because my computer, typically, was AWOL. The gates and windows had been closed!

However, as soon as I was back on line I heard from John Whitmarsh - yet another Don Quixote of the ether - that there was this strange, triffid-like site spreading further and wider, gathering poets and writers under its encouraging, warm foliage. And somewhere in the maw of this strange beast was a printing press!

That it was the brain-child of PC did not surprise me. She has a huge reservoir of ideas, a powerful determination to succeed, an immensely warm personality; and is about as organised as trouser-leg of ferrets.

So I volunteered to give her a hand in putting the site into some sort of logical order; which is slowly proceeding. But as I'm not much more organised myself, it's doubtless a nightmare to some of the writers. It will get better! Believe me. But the daily hordes at the gates make it a slow process!

For my own part, I've been writing (at first for my own catharsis) for about 20 years. After the initial period, I started writing for my own pleasure as well. But like many of us here, I've never had the confidence, the wit, the content or the determination to become published. However, Paula, with a background of publishing her own anthology, (and I hope many of you have bought a copy), has turned us into members of a kibbutz, for want of a better metaphor, and her judgement is law!

Before I was forty, only once did I write a piece of doggerel - at school, in response to a command in 'English'class. I can remember it to this day. "The young Princess of Furstenburg / Whose name was rather odd / Did meet by chance a wealthy Prince / Some think by Act of God".

I hope that I've progressed a bit further than that by now! So here's a piece of my own that you may not have seen: >>>>

AMPHIBIAN

Green-skinned, black-eyed, bloated Buddha,
Sceptical, sardonic and imperious of gaze,
Your bulk belies the catapult ability
Of your folded, flippered haunches.

No watcher would ignore
Your glowering, baleful glare,
Nor the inflation of your lungs
In rhythmic preparation of a belief-defying lunge,
Suggestive of pre-emptive acts of war.

It would be difficult to envy
Your amphibious career,
Your tiny, darting-tadpole twitch to life,
Your inherent air of evil;
For your appearance has the substance
Of dark, forbidding dreams.

Pete has been such a dedicated and hard-working member of the team
this year, that I had to give a section of the anthology over to him and his
work. Pete has also made a selection from the archive, shown below. Not
one to be missed! (Paula)

TEMPUS FUGIT

Francis Smith

Its time to go says the clock on the wall
At the end of a working day
Pick up your briefcase, put on your coat
You should no longer stay
Catch the tube or hail a cab and that's the final chore
Don't forget to turn the lock as you walk out through the door.
You've spent your life in this drab room toiling through the day
So pick yourself up and put on a smile
You should no longer stay.
From nine to five you struggled and strived, five days every week
No one said thank you or even well done, at least not so to speak.
Through spring and summer, autumn too and even in the snow
You dragged yourself from your warm bed, knowing you had to go.
Forty years on you've done your bit, bones aching in every way
So say goodbye and fare thee well
You should no longer stay.
Its time to go says the clock on the wall
The end of a working life
Pick up your trinkets, memories all, and the picture of your wife
A friend to all, a kindly soul in each and every way
But now you're sixty years of age
You should no longer stay.

The Peoples Poet Love Story

Do You Love Me?

Rebecca Smith

Do you love me?
Those four simple words.
A question, never-ending.
How can I ask it?

For I know you love me.
But there is a subtle difference,
Between love and love.
What, you may ask?

I know your love is deep and true,
My best and dearest friend.
But the love I desire goes deeper.
The love kisses were made for.

When you kiss me, sometimes,
I wonder if you know, at all,
How the kisses make me feel inside.
Warm, tender, and yet somehow scared.

Do you love me?
Do you understand what love I mean?
I am afraid of this love!
For what will it lead to, but a broken heart?

Can I tell you my love,
How I feel, my love?
Do you know, or realise,
How much I want your love?

What is Our Love?

Dave Seaman

What is our love, that so sudden has found us,
Against every hope, espied and thus bound us?
Through three years and more, fate has kept us apart;
A love that seemed lost to us, right from the start.
And now my true feelings to you are revealed;
A truth that by my lips forever was sealed.
Eaten up by passion, consumed by desire;
Hungering for your touch, my heart is on fire;
Thirsting for your kisses, my mind is ablaze;
A burning to last me for all of my days.
But flames not of torment, these were heaven-sent;
So this is what stories of true love all meant.
I know that your feelings to mine are akin;
We victors that never expected to win.
But the joy we have now, can it really last?
I feel that it can: uncertainty has past.
I love you with all my heart, body and soul,
Never on our love shall death sound out its'toll.

So Much In Love

Dave Seaman & Rebecca Smith

We're so much in love,
But how did it happen?
One day, just good friends,
The next filled with passion.

I looked in your eyes,
And suddenly I knew,
That my life had changed,
And all because of you.

My heart is now yours,
And yours belongs to me,
Forever entwined,
And ne'er parted to be.

How could I have known,
From that day we first met,
How time would unfold?
How destiny was set?

My darling, you know,
I'll love you forever.
To keep you happy,
I'll always endeavour.

We're so much in love,
Don't care how it happened.
Can't believe our luck,
In this fate we've fasioned.

Spotlight Polls

SARAH TRACY
She Promised

She writhes and fists her heaving chest
Her lungs are done, in need of rest
Imprisoned inside a world of hell
With rotting sores and sticky phlegm

The spears of pain sore through her back
Her body racks and hacks - a sack
Empty of things fresh and pure
Folds in pain, creases to floor

Her children weep in sorrow and pain
She said, she promised, again and again
Now the grave is dug and the body waits
She doesn't smoke now, but it's too late

SAMANTHA JONES
Dreamers

I see faces in the leaves and make patterns out of branches
I see just what I want to see, for this alone enhances
Images within in my mind of futuristic things
Making my life bearable, giving my heart wings
To fly so high above the clouds without a second glance
At pain and misery below, my mind is in a trance
I skim the mountains, chase the clouds across the sky so blue
Then suddenly return to earth...as all sad dreamers do

MIGUEL ANGEL BERRIOS

THE DIARY OF PAIN

Poetry can be so complicated, sometimes
when a man who has no voice, decides
to wear a mask of chronological inversion
for his sacred verses, he can no longer write.

Poetry can be so unusually painful
when you've lived all the unwritten lines.
And life, she offers you the gift of self expression
but you choose instead, to write these lies.

Poets can always be, breath to the dying
Who lie unconscious, unsuspecting in the grass.
But, what if I forget human emotions
Will they remember the pain that's in my heart?

Poetry;
a diary of greater success for empty readers.
Never mind the vocation of these lonely writers,
Heaven still holds a place for them, believers.

DEREK BATCHELOR

"Stony Bridge"

After hundreds of years in the making by nature
comes the setting, of a bridge over a stream,
So ideal and so perfect at the end of a lane
and at sunset so much like a dream.
At the end of a lane this bridge started life
wide enough for one car on its own,
The stories this bridge, such a cute little bridge
could tell were it not made of stone.

It was built with precision for its purpose intended
over years wore an ivy`s embrace,
Evening when the sun almost touched the horizon
this bridge always offered solace.
The playground of children for year after year
but now only from memory be seen,
For no longer is evidence of this, collection of words
can if ever be proved to have been.

The view of the stream flowing under the bridge
where the flight of the gnats entertain,
Was it then any wonder for those who love nature
to return here again and again.
The shallow little stream had for many an era
arched its back whilst meander through fields,
Not just running water with stones for its bed
but in awe for the life that it yields.

Like sticklebacks and larvae, small leaches and bugs
not to mention the dragonfly as well,
For the stream as the trees, that so long stood the banks
like the bridge many stories could tell.
But as I`ve said early on its only memory that paints
of a picture of which did exist,
After hundreds of years in the making by nature
its no longer a haven....just missed.

CHERYL CUNLIFFE
THE POT OF GOLD

Each one of us strives towards a goal
A dream of what could be
We each hold a thought of how things will go
But the clouds roll by & we get blown off course.

Between the gloomy clouds that shroud our happiness
A rainbow appears where tears & laughter collide
A cascade of colourful hope suddenly shines through
If we ride the rainbow will we find what we seek?

The pot of gold with its ray of joy
The glow of colour the thought of what's in store
Will we take a chance to find that ultimate dream?
Or will we slump back to the devil we know.

A kaleidoscope of life, which path to take?
Do we know what we want?
Find your dream & chase away the hurt
Life is full of surprises some happy some sad.

You know when you're riding your rainbow
Because hope makes your heart sing
You know when you've reached your pot of gold
When you look into his eyes & they smile golden rays of love!

JOHN WHITMARSH

Tempt Me At Forty
Was selected by Dave Seaman

GEOFF HOUGH
Legacy

I am the guardian of chronicles past,
The watcher at the gates of time.
Though kings have come, empires waned
And yet I steadfast vigil made.
To decide the memoried fates of men,
How the future will remember them.
Opening shutters for centuries passed.
Past windows lit for present rooms.

The fires of worlds long departed
 Still cast a glow in their tomorrows now,
I rake their bitter glorious embers;
Decide which coal to render brightest,
Which shall cool, and that detritus.
To search for reason amongst those ashes,
To venture truth from phoenix flames,
Consigning dross to times sad, piling heap.

Pinpoints candescent in dark times sky,
Searching black for destiny's men,
Traced events or trends of human hope.
 Dynasties of lights luminary grouped
In stark and twinkling constellation,
Linked by lines of war and conflagration.
To spy all this with future hindsight
Yet know your truth will not cost one single life.

I plot the ebbs and tides of nations,
Ships of state through storm raged stations.
Gales of fortune over gloried seas,
Crossing currents and winds of chance.
Of becalmed great empires stagnant bound
Lost within, besieged without.
To see with certainty wrong passage plied
And chart true course to have been laid.

And as evening's tired recalls the morning's toil,
As night's dream reflects the day's events;
So I bask in deliberate reason,
To review the past from Earth's late season.
Having walked with kings beyond my time
And seen the roads they knew not of
I stand at the gates of human knowledge
To guard it's future with portents from the past

Jörgen Jansson
TO HAVE AND TO HOLD

Curiosity has always been my guide...
Shows me the bright and free winds...
Blows me to the centre of my heart...
What can I say about the dreamteller?
It's all about the one final journey...
Leaving blues for the essence of love

Go with her a little further high
Calm breeze, she walks the water
Holds your love and plenty more
Believe her, she is coming home

To have and to hold
Feel your heart bumping around
Ask that question again
I can feel the flame in the room
To have and to hold
I can't make you do it this plain
To have and to hold
I know the emotion in your heart

Wisdom from the spirit won
Her love makes you stronger
This heart can heal your soul
Have you ever felt this before?

To have and to hold
Feel my heart dancing around
Ask that question again
I can feel the flame in the room
To have and to hold
I will make you do this again
To have and to hold
I know the emotion in this heart

PETE NIGHTINGALE
Rejection

Discarded feelings
Rot like leaves in the winter;
If love is the strongest
Of human emotions, in rejection
Its strength is its weakness.

As an insect is trapped
By minute strands of gossamer
Which glisten with dewdrops,
Love struggles amidst a glister of tears,
And may never break free.

STEVE TODD

FOR THE FALLEN

How sweet the air around the grave
of the weary Soldier, principle slave
of a Nation.
No-one knew him, no-one knew the freedom
he bought for wife, and self, and son.
No gentle filligree
to grace his headstone.

He died at home, a broken man.
Spurned by King and Country, and the name
of 'Soldier' meant no more than fleeting fame
in the early days.
For his Shade wanders by those other graves
of those who knew him not, for whom he fought.
The flowers of Flanders wither at the thought,
For peaceful sleep is all his spirit craves.

I knew you not, but knew you more than they!
Cry not in death, for you wept much in life.
Waste not your spectral tears on aged strife
but on those half-crazed fools who clash today.
They spill their blood while Politicians nod
They dedicate their massacres to God.
One half bade Peace; but they shall all know none
For like you, friend, their wasted lives are gone.

Cry tears for those who fell while under fools!
Cry tears for those who died to keep the rules!
Cry tears for children now who know no more
than lying hands-on-head upon the floor!
Be vigilant on high and blinded men
who smile, and smite a Country with a Pen.
Can you not see these Soldiers, long dead men,
Who writhe in silent screams of 'Why again?'

ANDREW SHISTON
Old Weymouth

As the tide floods the beaches
And the shear legs disappear
The Sprat boats leave their moorings
For another fishing year

Across the bay of Weymouth
In the early morning mist
The surface of the water
Shiver to diamonds from the fish

The Sprats they come in millions
You can catch them from the shore
Then the Sprat boats return loaded
To dock at Weymouth pier

As daylight fades to darkness
Across this special bay
Bright shapes break the surface
As the Mackerel come to stay

The fishermen and every boat
That can muster from the shore
Go out across the water
To angle and to trawl

No bait is ever needed
Just long and shiny hooks
They catch the fish in dozens
And land them in their boats

Now the years have passed
Across this Weymouth bay
The Spratting season comes to time
But the fish don't come this day

The trawlers and the Sprat boats
Stay tied up along the pier
And the fishermen are idle
For another fishing year.

Poetry Selected Online

Pictures in Words

Battles & Tears

Love

Story Telling

Nature

Art

Seasonal

Pictures in Words & Words in Pictures

The Elixir

Gareth Smith

Trickle down the window pane,
And settle in the gutter.
Drown in water you may find,
And take care not to splutter.
Pour yourself into a glass,
And serve it with a mixer.
Hide your own taste deep within,
And dole out this elixir.

Give in to the shifting seas,
And lose yourself to fashion.
Wash yourself in apathy,
And feelings you could ration.
Let your scent free once or twice,
And snare yourself a soul mate.
Try and use whatever's left,
And there you'll find it's too late.

The Graduate

Peter Nightingale

Hanging on the wall-
A portrait:
The eldest daughter,
Full of poise and presence,
Tall and slender;
The black, sharp lines
Of gown and mortar contrasting
Vividly with the clear,
Blue eyes;
The smile a broad amalgam
Of pride, embarrassment
And the fulfilled ambition of a goal achieved.

And grouped around her -
Three acolytes:
Beige-suited mother, seemingly
Herself hardly older than her first-born;
And two long-haired sisters:
Dark ringlets to her shoulders,
The one in white crossing the
Threshold of womanhood before her time,
Her beauty held forever, here, in bloom;
While the younger awakens in her teens,
olding the female promise
More clearly, even,
Than the three with whom she stands.

Three wide smiles of reflected glory:
But four family smiles - smiles
Bequeathed by the laughing
Grandad, loving father,
Whose major graduation
Was this framed certificate,
This four-fold, living legacy.

The Stately Homes of England
Geoff Hough 2002

Sentinel houses in grime-dirtied streets,
Brick upon brick, neat and complete.
Stately homes for the proud sons of toil,
Returning to rest from the grease and the oil.
Straight-up and sturdy, boxed side by side,
Purple-capped roofs break into the sky.
Uniform windows and regimental doors,
Green and cream painted - for one, as for all.
Donkey stoned steps prepared with such pride,
Done almost daily by bent-double wives.
Gatepost gossip and neighbourly news,
Fearsome matrons and outdoor loos.
Clacking, cobbled, careworn streets
That carried those tired returning feet.
Nearly all gone now, consigned to the past,
Terraced yet cherished, right to the last.

Beautiful Mum
Sarah Tracy

I wear stretchy jeans so they hold up my bum
And if they're a 12, they squeeze in my tum
I have soft, blonde hair - well, the soft bit's a lie
But I do have blonde hair - from a bottle of dye
I can't afford implants for boobs that are flat
I don't mind so much, they fed, and that's that
My hands will never be soft as my face
They really do dishes and clean up the place
I'll never be classed as a dish anymore
Gravity and age shut that open door
But hey! I've been there - I used to be wild
But now, my goal is a darling, grandchild
So please don't judge me, or think I'm a sap
'Cos I'm fattening my thighs for a big, cosy lap
My boys think I'm a most beautiful gal
That's me! Their mum! The one they call Sal

SWANSONG

David Savoury

In February and March, this year,
driving to work, I saw two swans
drifting on a flooded meadow's
tarnished silver, under a hedge
that straggled away towards a hill
where sluggish sheep cropped muddy grass.

The sky was buttermilk and pewter
with clouds, that looked like iron-wool,
cleansing the light into a cruel
brilliance on their folded wings,
white against the grey and sagey
greens of winter in the country.

Then I longed to see the city's
lights on pavements full of people
dodging traffic; going to parties,
drinking wine and swapping gossip
in restaurants, where the chandeliers
banished thoughts of creeping cold.

I wanted love, with scented candles
burning softly beside the bed;
wanted breakfast, lunch and dinner
in faux-French cafes, Edith-Piaf-
proof against all fond regrets:
against the cruel truth of swans.

The leaves are falling. Now I find
I want the winter and its cleansing
frosts, my darling: now you're gone
the country doesn't frighten me:
something tired discerns the beauty
of quiet water and a single swan.

"Blissful Night"
By Derek Batchelor

Tonight it seems I cannot sleep
so full my life today,
My room unlit my curtains wide
whilst sit my window bay.
Would surely be so black a night
yet daylight seems so soon,
As snow is falling just like feathers
against a silvery moon.

Nightime brings its change to colour
as definition is hardly slight,
The stencilled trees like ghostly figures
displayed in black and white.
Unlike the wind or even rain
so gentle is the snow,
One flake on flake throughout the night
its depth does surely grow.

Not long my eyes snow`s gentle fall
my mind so long to keep,
Instilled so surely of restful slumber
and much my needed sleep.
Can resist no more my tired eyes
to close or even fight,
Secure and warm my beds embrace
at last, will sleep the night.

Passing By
Sam Smith

Above the grey pavement,
moss mounding its cracks,
evening light picks out
clustered green-gold seeds
of a tall garden ash.
Spilling out from
a closing pub door
are men's hardened voices
and the smell of beer.

An impossibility,
in an imperfect world,
to perfect oneself.
The wise, therefore,
believe in contradictions,
embrace mixed feelings.

Beyond dark angled rooftops
fawn and pink clouds
make a jig-saw of the sky.
On the ink-blue corner
young men hang about to
practise their spitting.

Unwise
wherever I have so far been
people
have got in the way of the view.

Battles & Tears

All Different All Equal.

Yvette Hawkins

Would you judge me
If I told you
I held a grudge against
All of those to whom I judge?
And would you give a damn at what I can
And cannot do
To you?
I am nobody.

Somebody who believes
In a world of perfect hue
Cannot exist in an
Unfolding
Imploding
Corroding reality
Absorbed within their perfect vanity.

So judge me
Grudge me
Try to touch me
Disrupt my soul
An equal practically
Perfect mould to fit your view
But deep inside I'll mould the truth
We are the same
I am you
I will judge you
And I will grudge you
I'll stick to my opinion
I'll never budge
And see that I am as right as you
Absorbed within this perfect hue
For me to continue to
Ever grudge you
Will always end up with me to
Judge you.
You'll give as good as you can take
And just as much
But fuck
When did anyone give
Anyone else
The right
To judge.

The Third Son
John J Whitmarsh

The third son of the standard serf family
Is said, in fairytales Grimm and Anderson,
To shine with the light of dreams realised,
Thus it was no surprise when he
Won the hand of Maiden Fair and
Shared her father's kingdom after
Ridding it of dragons, ogres and Black Knights,
Nor were we shocked to learn that
The fields heaved with corn at his behest
Or that orchards showered apples
To the fattening pigs and goats lazing there.
Houses sprang from hovels,
Labourers grew strong and smiles
Lit up the sun-bright days of skipping little girls
And would-be, will-be hero boys.
But an error in the final chapter,
A misprint, a slip, an editor's oversight
Or a vicious author's warped sense of fun
Deprived the reader of a happy-ever-after,
For the laughter stopped when the
Handsome prince rode by, tense with pain,
In a far too real
Wheelchair.

Give or Take
Samantha Jones

Life is full of takers...the givers stay behind
Discreetly in the background, the ones you'll never find
Perhaps I'll find a giver, who understands my need
Instead of only takers...my very soul to bleed

A Letter, Unposted
Peter Nightingale

To:
Foetus, part-formed,
far too tiny.

"Never knew you the love of your father.
But he knew of you. And denied you."

From:
Male, self-centred
Far, far too late.

I WAS SOMEONE
MIGUEL ANGEL

"The darkest night approaches"

Even though I am still standing
in the middle of the desert.
There are the unknown traces

of the time I was somebody.
"The darkest night approaches"

And it is not the distance,
nor the chance of drowning.
It is the lasting mornings
that never become instants.

"The darkest night is closer"

I was a glimpse of glory
that you made of your own.
And I could have deeply sworn
you were a different story.

"The darkest night approaches"

I am here still, and voices
remind me I was once, someone.
Like a prince of Egypt own hands,
before they became Moses'.

"The darkest night approaches"

Unbridgeable Distances

Alan Corkish

...some things never change
the distance between
you and i
for example
is
197 miles exactly
as is
the distance between
me and you
easily do it in four hours
even with a generous
smoke-break...

but the distance between
you and i
is also
19 years...
19 years
of political life

..maybe,
without a generous
smoke break,
we
could bridge   that gap
given time...

but
the **real** distance
between you
and i
is as insurmountable
and unbridgeable as
the recent silences
that dogged
our lonely
togetherness...

Bakersfield Beat

John Whitmarsh

In a tumbleweed town where the oil well is king,
Where the bottle is god for them all,
She dances away to the beat of her blood,
In a lonely and personal ball.

She dances all night to the beat of her blood
With a rhythm that's heavy and dull,
Wishing her man would come along soon,
She dances her life all alone.

To the throbbing of wind and the pounding of rain,
She follows her heartbeat's lead,
Just filling the hours with the mad splash of life,
In the ballroom inside her head.

Way out to the bluffs above the wild creek
In her tumbleweed dance of defiance,
She searches the shadows more real than her life,
And discovers a terrible silence.

The oil wells are hushed and the air has turned cold
And the beat of her blood is stilled;
She curses the town where the tumbleweed rolls,
Where the magic of life is killed.

She sits on a rock where the lichen grows thick
And takes one last slow-motion breath,
Then tumbleweeds down to the boulders below
In a last graceful waltz to her death.

The Patio
Ricky Kane

As I silently watch you on the patio,
From the kitchen where I am sat,
I catch a glimpse of myself in the window.
The humourless, haggard face that looks back is
A reflection of my present.
A remberance of my past.

A past of you sieving Shakespeare into comprehensive kids'
Minds. A past of me building that bloody patio.
You thought were always above me
In your self: The queen of comprehensive.
For you it was Love's Labours Lost
For me, labour lost my love.

The labour of living the lies that lay the
Foundation of our life.
The labour of forging friendships with those
At the PTA. A forgery of friendships.
The labour of disregarding the dashing Mr.
'Design and Technology'as a mistake.
And the labour of building that bloody patio, burying the earth with slates,
As if it were our true past being tainted by the tiled tiredness of life.

As I silently watch you on the patio,
From the kitchen where I am sat,
I catch a glimpse of the sun, shining radiantly
Upon your face. And as I watch you rest on the patio,
I can't help but feel:
How much better you'd look underneath it.

Another Generation
Helen Parkes

I was talking to my friend today, because she was feeling blue
I told her to take a look around, smell the flowers, take in the view.

With luxuries in every family, we live in extravagant ease
machines to do everything for us, and we're still so hard to please.

A car to every worker, heating to every home
Cable TV, computer games, video players and a mobile phone!

If we are lacking in one, we are a failure; we strive to have works
when we have it, we still want more, to add to our self worth.

Our credibility and self-esteem, is governed by the latest fad
no wonder we all feel stressed, we're driving ourselves mad!

I'm sitting here, smelling the flowers, taking in the view,
thinking of generations before, which had good reason to feel blue...

Colour of Your Tears
Francis Smith

Well, Biafra
What colour are your tears today?
Did God forget your pain and frighten you away?
As all the world joined in this sad refrain

Then crying false emotion
dug deep into their pockets once again
In Ethiopia, Afghanistan and Ireland too
These tears that flow are called a different name

And yet they're all the same
With eyes too dry in sorrow as you in anguish cry
When praying to your Gods
And swiftly die.

These Feelings I Have
Gareth Smith

These feelings I have,
No words can express.
This stillness of heart,
This grief I suppress.

The thunder and storms,
That rage in my head,
Are kept from the door,
And swallowed instead.

One day I'll give in,
My armour will crack,
And all of the pain,
Will come tumbling back.

When my house falls down,
And the past takes hold,
I'll cry all my tears,
Relinquish control.

Lonesome
Jose Luis Lopez

Walking through a night
I saw the stars up the sky
they blinked like flashy eyes
flattering my heart.

Brushing the sand around
with my satin feet
drawing a girl in shadows
who'll look at me.

Even the sea helped me
painting the body and eyes
I wish she would've lived
when I kissed on her lips.

That did not happen
winds vanished all over
now my breath went away
she couldn't live any longer.

I'm lonesome
not for her, not for me
someday life will create
another being to love with.

I'm lonesome
not forever, but somehow
destiny will set up for me
with joy, peace and eternity.

A SHORT COMMENTARY
Miguel Angel

When I am distant and chaotic
murmur, those words you dearly keep.
In your chest, they mean nothing unless spoken
and when spoken, they lose their power to heal.
For the waters, they all die when in the ocean
and the sun, dies alone when in the night;
shadows wear the mask of sweet conviction
as if knowing it has finally lost its might.

The Face at the window
Samantha Jones

See the face at the window, with a sadness in her eyes
Watch her follow every movement of the clouds across the skies
It looks as if she's searching for a dream that cannot be
Just longing to escape and like the birds fly free
Alas, she's caught up in her pain, see it etched upon her face
Staring out with haunting eyes, gazing into space
Why does she look familiar, her reflection I can see
I look again through that window and the haunted face is me

Through the eyes of a Martyr
©Dragonslayer Tyu 2001 S.Helps

Flames envelop me,
Darkness surrounds me,
I struggle to fight for my beliefs,
The insane battle between two sides,
Fighting for succession,
To win,
To destroy all obstacles to victory.

Death,
Blood,
Desolate landscapes,
Destruction,
This is all that is left from my struggle.

~Fin~

STOP

Cheryl Cunliffe

Cancel everything, my life standing still
My world collapsed last night I've lost my will.

Can't face the world outside my door
Afraid, alone, it doesn't matter anymore.

Don't want to talk, just write a message or two
You see I know what I saw is true.

But it's not for me to say or sort
I hope that they'll realise and be pulled up short.

You said I'd have to be Jesus at the mo
But can it stop now it hurts just so.

Can't breathe or eat
Please Lord it's an uncomfortable seat.

Can't remember what this is all for
I don't want to be a pawn whilst you settle the score.

Enough already I'm drained
Can't move, every part of me strained.

ONE did make a difference, a spear through the heart
Why Lord do I have to be set apart.

One day I felt on a mountain top
Now I just want the world to **STOP**!!

WEEPING WILLOW

Lucy Garrard

Weeping Willow
Listen to the silence that screams
As I lay in my grave
Listen to my heart thumping
In the dark
Watch me pray for tomorrow
And laugh.
Can you hear the noise of today
That I wish I would just die?
Weeping Willow
Follow the footsteps in my heart
That make me who I am
And what I feel
Watch my slow agonizing dance
That never ends
And wonder when.
Weeping Willow
Ask me the questions on your mind
But please don't judge.
Reach for my hand
But don't touch me yet
Watch me laugh with my friends
Can you hear me screaming
In the crowd?
Weeping Willow
Follow my childhood trails
For the answers to the noise.
Question him
For the key to the door
Listen to the voices of the past
Can you see my frozen tear?
Weeping Willow
Feel the delightful edges
To my disappearing soul,-
My challenge.
Watch me shed my reptile skin
To reveal a graceful swan.
Listen to the silence that screams
Can you see me suffer
Until I hear a noise?
Watch my slow agonizing dance....halt.
And wonder when.
Weeping Willow
Help me breathe again.

DRINK or BACCHUS SONG

STEVE TODD

Drink!
Drink to the health of your sins!
Drink for the War-No-One-Wins!
Drink!

Drink!
Drown the widows of woe!
Drink to the ways you may go!
Drink!

Drink!
For to drink is a fine way to die!
With a nod, and a word, and a sigh!
Drink!

Drink!
For the average is more than the most!
And reality, only a ghost!
Drink!

Drink!
For love is a fickle thing!
Bound up with hope and a ring!
Drink!

Drink!
For the time to be different is through,
And love is a fickle thing,
And the average is more than the most,
And reality, only a ghost,
And to not, a prelude to a sting!
Drink!

BLOCKED OUT

Jörgen Jansson

I've sold the book of love now
I've picked up the present time
My funeral was no pretty sight
An empty yard filled by ghosts

I had to give it all up and count back
I was moving fast back down the line
I really need to find a stepping stone
Move from these worn out mindfields

I've been blocked out in my shadow
Seen myself from the doomed side
I've been blocked out in my shadow
Left behind my world of religion
A hidden light in my own shadow
Blocked out the spirit of a man

The big fiction has been my space
between self deception and reality
I hold the walls from falling down
The game of trivial pursuit I won

Now I feel the sense and sensibility
The rational response is happening
Moving out from a nebula of insanity
Starting up in my own world of light

I've been blocked out in my shadow
Seen myself from the doomed side
I've been blocked out in my shadow
Left behind my world of religion
A hidden light in my own shadow
Blocked out the spirit of a man

The spirit of a man is back with confidence
The spirit of the man holds the eternal light
All the shadows will surely follow in his wake
All the shadows will fall into the eternal light

I'm Coming Home

Andrew A Hide

I've been away for many years,
I've waded through mud, blood and tears,
in foreign lands I faced my fears,
and now I'm coming home.

I've seen the innocent cry in pain,
I've seen the guilty die in shame,
I've seen homes burn down in flame,
and now I'm coming home.

Just down this street, my house in view,
this cherished home that I once knew,
but all around seems so new,
and now I'm coming home.

Will you still hold me in your arms?
Present me with a lovers charms?
When I feel angry, make me calm?
Because now I'm coming home.

I'm not the man I used to be,
my body has scars, as you will see,
my minds scarred too, no longer free,
and now I'm coming home.

My comrades in arms, in fields they fell,
in the name of peace we marched into hell,
I'm not the same man inside this shell,
but at least I made it home.

Not A Day Goes By
Pete Nightingale

Not a day goes by
But I think of you.

Not a day goes by
But I grieve for you.

Not a day goes by
But I yearn for you.

Not a day goes by;
No -
Not a day goes by.

Depression
Dan Walker

No light
No sun
No warmth
No fun
No faith
No love
No God
Above
No joy
No hope
So hard
To cope
DEPRESSION

Listen
Paula Cleife

Listen to the girl,
The childish girl in
The pathetic pigtails.
What does she know?

What does she know
Of life,
Of love,
Of success?

Isn't she just stupid
With a heart full of love
And dreams of making the World listen
To the sound of her energy?

What does she know
Of weariness,
Sickness,
Of pain?

Isn't she naive,
Thinking she will succeed
On nothing but a good idea
And people who love her?

What does she know
Of loneliness,
Failure,
And fear?

Are you afraid
Of what might happen
If you just
Stop..
And listen to the girl?

SADNESS
Cheryl Cunliffe

My world fell apart the day you said goodbye,
I felt hurt and deceived was it all a lie?

The sadness fell like the curtain on a stage,
And my heart broke and I filled up with rage.

I plead with the phone to ring with your voice,
You decided to leave I never had a choice.

As the night falls,
My heart calls.

I wish you could see,
All the riches in me.

With sadness I sit,
Contemplating my bit.

I just want you back again,
Holding and comforting me, making the sadness go away.

Abandoned, alone, sadness and fear,
I wish I could see a way that's clear.

Of letting go and going through,
I really love you, of this I know is true.

But a sadness is gripped,
And my heart is ripped.

Tell me how you feel,
Was us ever real?

Sadness….it's just a word,
It just describes me I'm scared!

EX SOCIAL SERVICEMAN
Carlton Hunt

The major, gleaming medals pinned on blazer,
Raw back and sides with a cutthroat razor,
What reward did his valor earn?
Another visit from Age concern.

For king and country, the right thing to do,
His battle now rages in the bus queue,
What did he get for a nation's defence?
A leaflet on incontinence.

The star of the Burma boys, one man per sleeper,
Stiff upper lip, the dreadful secrets keeper,
What did he get on a veteran's pension?
To pay for the Jubilee line extension.

A member of the disarmed forces,
All the kings'men, without the horses,
Bullied beef and powdered eggs,
He'd chase the little blighters,

But he's got no legs.
The poppies, the legion, the just and true cause,
The shriveled up heroes of two world wars.

Misty Today
R.J. Miller

The mist in my head,
Just wont go away,
It's clouding my thoughts,
In every which way.
It's there in the morning,
And still there at night,
This mist in my head,
Is clouding my sight.
I once saw things clearly,
And everything looked bright,
Then you came in to my life,
And dimmed the light.
You changed the way I felt,
And made me worship you,
You changed everything about me,
And put my life in a stew.
But then they came and took you,
They had to put you away,
Free once again to live my own life,
Things will improve but it's misty today.

Listen 2 me
anthony beechey

The old lady sits on the other side of the street
brushing her hair with her hands
the wrinkles decay the beauty of the forgotten years
the lady speaks out
a cry of despair
listen to me, just listen to me

the paralyzed man sits and observes
the hustle bustle of human life
the crowds walk past
cries of laughter and joy
the despair in his heart
saying listen to me, just listen to me

The man on the stage
the look in his eye
his words speak such volumes
when they are spoken
they are lost and battered by storms of frustration

The man sings his song
the frustration has gone
the silent tears well up in his eyes
there's no despair,
no suffering, just care
the cries of mercy and grace

listen to me, can you all see
there are talents that bubble inside
listen to him and you will know
the angel of love is inside

Monsoon of blood

John J Whitmarsh

Is this pitiful knife all that remains
Of the adventure that was to change my life,
All that my voyage to pastures new has to offer me?
What a lie is love! – the emotion reputed to put light into stars
And shine in the petals of dew-laden roses!
No roses for me today –
I have the impressions of thorns scratched deep
And eternal to mark my daring, failed excursion.

Where was the scented bower? The arbour with butterflies?
The marble-pillared portico
With cushioned seats for us to spoon upon?
In a hotel room, that's where! –
With blinds pulled over,
And a 'Do not disturb'sign hurriedly hung outside.
Needless to say, I consider Cupid's modelling of my days
To be the work of an inept and clumsy amateur.

But I live and learn – I learn to overcome my acid grief or,
Failing that, to hide it unconvincingly behind this bolted door.
No more need I wonder what to wear,
What make-up to apply, how soon to leave to meet him –
For I have the ticket now, and I will use it when the phone rings –
And I will answer his charming 'How are you?'
With a satisfying
'I am dying.'

A Facade
Michele Schofield

A fountain of eloquence,
The words that you speak.
The truth in your lies,
The love that you seek.
The words are so shallow,
Just a mask that you wear,
And if it ended tomorrow,
Would your 'fans'still wait there?
The world is your stage,
As you speak of a love,
This undying devotion,
And the heavens above.
They listen with rapture,
To all that you say,
They ask for your blessing,
As they kneel down to pray.
But where are your friends,
As you climbed to the top?
Did you trample upon them,
Never pausing to stop?
Did you become deaf,
From fortune and fame?
Can you still hear a pauper,
If he calls out your name?
Are the diamonds around you,
Only blinding your eyes?
To the pain that you cause,
The tears and the sighs.
You think you have love,
For you paid them to care.
But if you look closely,
You'll find no one is there.
So stand tall at the top,
Wearing jewels in your crown.
You left love at the bottom,
Should you ever come down.

Weary
Amy Baldry

A weary sun rises to a new day.
A virgin screams at old horrors,
And now we are gathered
Like cats before a storm.

A new moon shines on a weary world
And the sinner shies from the light.
They leave to us this land,
A land that we do not want.

Constant waves crash on old shores,
Like time on open woumds.
Generations memories flood
Back into our eyes.

Death echoes in the raging wind
And soldier's tears norish
The now red soil,
That screams from lack of air.

Empty faces and skeleton children
Run wild in the streets,
With empty bellies and empty hearts
And a chest full of hope.

A new cry, born to the dying.
A new sun rises on a new day
And we reach for the light
As we shy from the belly of darkness.

Heaven's Tear
D. R. Hurford

Faces in clouds, they weep for relief,
and shower in tears, my being, my keep.
Do you cry for me? My Lord in release?
Is this crying for me?
Now I lay here so weak?

Speak wisdom in winds, in my hour of need.
And blow strong to clear, my demons, these sleeps.
How pretentious of me, that I should believe,
that your winds are for me,
God, I lay here so weak.

Callings in dreams; this one's on his knees,
but tell me one thing:
Are these bells in your raindrops, that chime on release,
the last song for someone? For someone?
For me?

SO MUCH MEAT
Paul White

Instrumental in dripping tortuous echoes of my mind
I feel the wax begin to melt beneath my feet
And all in all the purest darkest vision I could find
Was viewing there the world as so much meat

An abattoir of friends and faces arching with desire
Towards the very blackened heart they'd ever know
But who am I to turn away those souls destined for fire?
And who are they to think they'd never go?

To be called by a stranger's name is something never heard
When all who come to reckoning are guilty there
I feel your loins are aching then with punishments deserved
Still pleading upon ears that never care

I tear your soul into the parts that make the human clay
And mould your inner feelings into deadened lead
Create the purest flour from the goodness tossed away
And make you wish that you were never dead

Fragments of a child
Amy Baldry

I am in the roots of the tree
That sways outside my window
Reminding me when, as a child,
I would with trifling steps
Rest in its grey shadow.

I am in the soil that gravely cradles
Life and death, caressing the bones
Of childhood treasures
Entombed in stone and memory.

Fragments of a smile are hidden in these walls.
My tears, my hopes are fossilised
In layers of time
Perserved by innocent love.

I live in forgotten corners, where
Old dreams echo in the darkness.
I breath in sweetened air
And hide in soft shades
Untouched by times fast hands.

I am immersed in virgin tears
That haunt me in the now heavy clouds
That tower over me,
Threatening to drown the sun.

Story Telling

The Human Race

Scott Tyrrell

So I asked this guy to my left,
Where we were running to.
He said he didn't know,
It just seemed the thing to do.

So I asked the girl to my right,
"Where are we running to?"
She just shrugged her shoulders
She didn't have a clue.

So I asked the guy behind me,
"Look, where are we running to?"
He gave me a funny look
And he said "I'm following you."

So I asked the girl in front,
"Do you know where we're going?"
She said, "I don't know about you,
But I'm going where the wind is blowing!"

So I looked up at the wind,
"You must know where this journey ends?"
It said, "I'm following you lot,
I try to keep up with the trends."

I figured someone must know where we're headed
So I started to pick up the pace.
I ran faster and faster
I had to know who was leading the race.

In the distance I saw on old man
I cried to him, "What's up ahead?"
He turned around to see who spoke
And then he fell over

Dead.

I stopped at where he had fallen.
Now we were really in a mess.
"What do we do now?" someone cried.

"Well, we just keep running I guess."

Conversation On The Ward

John J Whitmarsh

I'm only crying till my mummy comes:
It is cold in here
And the injections hurt,
And I get frightened when they ask me questions
And use words like symptoms.
Most times, my head aches –
And my stomach feels hard,
And I was sick four times yesterday
And twice just now.
That nurse is a cow – the thin one –
She shouted at me and called me naughty,
And somewhere behind me there's a buzzer
For telling them when I need a wee,
But I can't find it – I think they hide it.
And they keep telling me to swallow big pills
Even though they know they make me choke,
And that girl over there hates me
Because she just came in yesterday
While I've been here all week.
I don't like it here on the kids'ward on my own.
I want to go home.
I miss my house with my things in it
And I miss my brother and my rabbit,
And most of all I miss being in my own bed.
But I'm only crying till my mummy comes.

Milton Keynes Station

Alan Corkish

(10/06/01)

she is crying

he grips his holdall
in one hand
caressing her shoulder
with the other...
lips meet softly
and no words escape
as they part

when she walks away
i have a bet
that she'll look back
and wave...
she does neither

later
pulling into Watford
as i return to my seat
with coffee
i pass him on his mobile...

he is laughing

S . I . W .

Alan Corkish

...they shoot themselves in the foot
you know
when the going gets tough
or shock reduces them to
tired shells...
it's to win the right to
return home honoured
(if they aint found out)

...from my Spanish
                 Uncivil War
i returned unhonoured...
nothing could hide
the blatant bloodied foot
the self-inflicted-wound
the coward's mantel...
no mock-honours even sort...
instead;
i sat on my hotel bed
dredged in a sort of
ignominy
and yet
feeling that i-did-as-i-had-to-do
feeling
i need no forgiveness for this
self-preserving
action
for not being
the man i knew i wasn't
            anyway...

Pathetic

© *Scott Tyrrell April 2002*

I'd like to ask you out
But you're better looking than me
And looks count for everything
In this society
I have a sense of humour
You say that's worth a lot
But Ken Dodd
Over Russell Crowe?
I think not.

The world's become skin deep
It's a superficial place
It seems to gang up
On those with a hang up
With their body and their face

But I'd love to be your lover
love to give you my all
But I'm embarrassed about me love handles
And I think me willy's too small
Well, it looks so silly
And I'm worried about the stem
I read it should be wider
In FHM.
And I ain't that pretty
And I stutter under pressure
And I feel like a fresher
In your university.
You intimidate me
But it's not you, you see
It's me, me, me
Says Woman's Weekly.

It's pathetic really
You could only say no,
But you might get upset
And you might shout and bellow,
And even worse than that
You might say you're flattered
Then string me along,
I'd be emotionally battered
Or you might move in
And then clean out my flat
Then fill it full of shite
From Habitat.

Or even Ikea
Now there's an idea
(I hear that bean bags
Are in this year.)

Oh, why can't this be easy?
I think I'm thinking too much
Oh I wish was good looking,
Not cuddly, but butch
And I wish I was cool
Like Starski and Hutch
And now I've
Built this up too much.

I'll leave it till another day
Until I've calmed down
But then someone else might ask you out
I'd feel like such a clown
Should I be spontaneous?
Dear Deirdre thinks I should
But this week Venus is in the cusp of Aries
So that's no good.

I should do what I feel is right
Not listen to that shite
After all I am an individual
With heart and soul and might
I don't have to follow trends
I am my own man!
At least, that's what it said
In Cosmopolitan.

Reminder

Scott Tyrrell

I walked up a hill in Winter.
I saw a robin cut clean
Through the wind and snow
And disappear into the mist
That settled over frosted dales.
Then I slipped on a patch of ice
And fell painfully on my arse.
I needed both to remind me of who I am.

GLASTONBURY TOR

Pete Nightingale

Seen distantly,
The eyes and thoughts are drawn persistently
To this ancient, noble pinnacle;
There can be no refusal
To respond to its low, persuasive call.

It is early spring.
Listen to the song of birds, which sing
Not just of now, but of the past they know,
Of the surging centuries which flow
So fast but still beneath the earth below.

Even God himself would strain his mind
To enumerate and illustrate
Such a pulsing throng of human kind,
Whose unnumbered feet have trod this hill;
Whose unnumbered eyes interpreted with skill
This all-encompassing, entrancing view.

And here are paramount
No binoculars or telescopes –
Which those unsighted raise
With eternal expectation
To their cataracted, granite eyes;
For were they but aware,
They need only to inhale – of an air
So pure – to sense the distillation
Of each preceding generation.

But also, here, the blind barbaric armies
Of an ambitious, reforming king
Hung, drew and quartered
A gentle abbot
– his gentleness was in his very calling.
From here, as death drew near, he perceived
The blue-bright promised skies
As his bequest, and embracing death, believed.

Unfettered from the chains of mortal agonies
At the last his soul escaped;
For the moment fragile, it fluttered free; and flew.
Just as these birds, now,
With their slow, enduring certainty,
Encircle endlessly,
Singing ancient messages – anew.

Dedicated to Richard Whiting, the last Abbot
of Glastonbury, executed for his faith in 1539.

ALL THINGS BRIGHTON BEAUTIFUL

Carlton Hunt

Her future was bright lights
With home town rejected
Lived it up for two weeks
At the hotel Majestic

To keep herself legal
She moved on to the Regal
Waking to the sound of
 Shrieking, starving seagulls

Living from mouth to hand
She eloped to the Strand
The sheets are purple nylon
Full of yesterdays sand

As a last resort
Holed up in the Connaught
Ignoring the doorbell
Trying not to get caught

Etched in the fluorescent glow
Outside the closed family fun show
The bed and breakfast children didn't know
Swimming against the raw sewage out flow

One girl in a million
Found dead in the pavilion
Her parents never knew
Why she took the sea view

Oh we do like to be beside the graveside

Birkenhead Lower Park

Alan Corkish

[26th Jan 2001]
There are no lovers in lower park.
Too young mothers and
too old prams,
the purposeless amble
of solitary males and
a Burns'hangover sitting
heavy on the brow of a
listless angler.
Ducks circle unfed
amongst thinly filmed
debris and jetsamed plastic
carriers,
Canada geese and a solitary swan
beak at a Tenants'can
by the scuffed blue bridge
with its biscuit broken
roof tiles.
And though I lingered for
an hour
and tried to communicate with
the demented fat man
with the too tight
black wool skull cap
which creased his brain
and made him
speak in tongues...
on this day,
    there are no lovers in lower park.

Abortion (October 1963)

Alan Corkish

Shut off from reality
and heavy with dark rum i guided her
to the house on
the hill where the
grotesquely humorous Dr Hook
waited with his
torn sheets and cotton
wool - hot-water and that
fisherman's knife with the
brass clasp that made her recoil
into my arms
Gagging with the fumes
from the pad i stood above her
and held one hand stifling
her screams with that
vomit-inducing ether
for close to two hours until
his eyes dark and fear-filled
told me it was over.
Afterwards i filled the carrier bags
with blooded scraps as she
laced a cotton pad between her
legs rocking... retching...
hand-on-distended-stomach
and then i picked up
a tiny globule and wiped it clean
perfectly curled in that
foetal position
three inches long
with sightless balls for eyes
and perfect toes and fingers...
Now; forty years on
i see it still; its eyes now
are blue and can see
the real me, the one who
planned and... executed...
There is no point in refusing
to accept
in arguing that i am
not he, reasoning that he
has gone totally,
every atom and molecule...
for i know that something
intangible is still the same and
so i accept the accusing stare
a reminder of the continuity
of my life and the finality of its.

Rest Home Daydreams- Christmas 1958.

STEVE TODD

In twelve days, a Christmas.
A new breath for tired shops,
New sights flooding cataract eyes
renewing a jaded child.

Darkened streets lit up
with the glow of rosy neon lights.
Your photograph, warm love
nestling in my colder hands.

Image of joy,
Snowblind, we laughed,
and threw rough snowballs.
Those days are gone now.

Chimneys, too small for an old
hope to traverse.
Pillow damp with new tears.
You are gone.

But still here, as the snow falls.
Inside the snug, cozy cottage of memory
We are still together.
The past will be my Present.

MY POTATO

Ricky Kane

Since you've gone you've left me cold.
And you've taken all the food.
All I've got left are the memories
..and this potato.

My heart is bare and empty,
The cobwebs keep it warm,
Like the larder that you too cleaned out
...but I've got the potato.

You can try and peel me down,
Slice, dice and fry in fat.
Then just for fun – bite mre in two,
..but leave my potato out of this.

MY PLACE
Karl Graham

I have an acre of land "No trespassing allowed"
It sits between an ocean and a sea
The view from this plot is out of this world
Would you care to come sit with me?

Next time you're heading to your dreams
Come to me and take my hand
I shall lead you the 238,900 miles
To my piece of lunar land

We can sit in peace watching our world as it spins
And wave to the people we know
Watch deep blue oceans,red sandy deserts
And the mountains topped with snow

We can't stay in this place forever
We must return to our bodies to awake
But this is my plot and i'll return
For the view,for peace and for sanity's sake.

Sandwiches For Two
John J Whitmarsh

Nothing stirred
In her humdrum days
To take away
The grey-on-grey,
The autopilot,
The wander-in-a mist mood -

And she was left to conclude
That her passing life
Was sweeping by
Without ebb or floe,
Bereft of tide
Or a candle's flickering light -

Until one night
She glanced along
The supermarket aisle
And saw a smile
That was aimed at her -
She smiled back, then fled,

With her wax-wrapped
Loaf of half-stale bread,
To the flat she shared
With her stereo -
And she vowed that, tomorrow night,
She would cut sandwiches for two.

"Drowned"

Andrew Shiston

From many fathoms deep below
In the dark and dismal depths
Where day and sunlight disappear
Lays a rusting rotten wreck
The weeds that grow upon her deck
Where seamen used to splice
Move like gentle pennants
Where proud flags used to fly
The only men that crew this wreck
That lays upon her side
Is a pile of rotting human bones
Of men that sailed and died.....

The Epic Of The Shipwrecked Sailor

Steve Todd

I. Abased and unique drifted I for days
Upon th'inviolate ocean, cold and moist
between the toes of my malnourished feet.
The Sun had rose and sank four times before
I moaned ultimatum to my hunger;
'Desist or...'('cook and eat me'died on breath)

At the Worlds edge the campfires brightly blazed
Complex signals. For me! To small boys, this were
no mean feat! They surely were
Small boys like angels, for they found me shore
And helped me to their makeshift camp, and fed
my weather'd body 'til it bulged

And strained the seams of my poor rag constraints
that pinched me as they dried. This multitude of
boys were NOT boys- nor men at all. Rather
they were in-between such growth.
Clothed in green, like sailors...atrophied.

Yet most silent. Mindful of their condition.
Fitful stares, and limps and blister'd faces.
When I regained my vigour, I asked them
'Who be you creatures? Tell me of thyself!
My appetite for food you sate, not knowledge'.

One said his name was Pipkin, and spoke up
'We once were men- now' beast-made-men- some say.
Some call us Leprechauns or 'Leper-Corns'.
The latter suits us, for you risk your skin
in staying with us. You are surely ours!'

'How dare you rescue me, O little men,
Then claim me as thy prisoner by Fate!
Hast thou no mercy, hast thou grown so sour
that every luckless, shipwrecked soul you see
Be ever caged in this community?'

They doffed their caps as one, and bid me sit
(For much alarmed I stood, within their midst).
'Dear Sir, beseech you! Take thy seat and hark
Our story is a dark and bitter one
thou shalt hold want to falsehood, but believe.'

One by one, the tale, divided up,
was laid before me to my disbelief.
Had not their earnest glares coerced my sense
I would have laughed, and branded it fantastical.

II. 'Two hundred years unto this very day
We few, we sullen few, were just as thee-
Fit and strong and cast in normal face
Contented, 'til our ship was lost at sea.'

'Good shipmates of the freighter VEILS OF LIGHT
We clung to wreckage, floating as our hope
That we'd survive the fury of the storm
While our charge, smash'd and batter'd, bit a reef.'

'For days we drifted, just as thoud didst drift
Until, somehow, we found the lip of th'sea..
None but twelve survived to make it here;
How strange- nay, how appalling the sour mercy!'

III. 'We beached ourselves, our limbs praising the sand
and gathered rigging ropes and barrels, all
that had been brothers to us those foul times,
then organised a hasty hunt for food.'

'We skewered a wild pig with a vulgar spear
that Reilly fashioned from our ship's nameplate.'
So saying, the crowd parted round the fellow
Who placed his head in hands and sobbed his piece;

'The spirit of our ship was displeased
by it's cold furied murder, sank and rent.
By blooding up it's name it came aroused
from those dead timbers, once a happy home

And realised it's end, it's unmarked grave!
It then possessed the Pig. In it's last throes
it voiced a curse at we bedraggled fools
for violation of the goodship's soul.'

'We shared the pork amongst ourselves, and ate.
Half-crazed,and ripping uncooked flesh with teeth,
We cursed the damned existence of that reef
and whisper'd in our worry of the hate

In which the swine had cursed us, in our tongue,
With force but held by truly righteous foes
whom retribution is a cousin to, and vengeance
a tag for a raw meal of men.'

'We slept as spent men sleep that night;
The uncooked animal we had consumed
in bloodied frenzy surely saved our lives.
But no, but no...for then there came the light.

'Come early morning, screams were all the air!
Some daemon saw us in our blood-soaked slumber
Destroyed our looks- for we'd been wond'rous fair-
and left us, monsters, wrapped in filthy skin.'

'Disfigured so as to shock e'en the blind!
Even our ageing, there, was dealigned!
And thus we stand before you as we are;
Alone in exile for our sin, forever.'

IV. 'Bravo! A worthy tale'I then replied
'This curse, though, lies on you and only you.
Behold! Iam not thralled; the same outside
as when you rescued me, and I arrived.'

'You wish to go? Begone!'They clamour'd round
And shoved me to their raft, a sturdy Sail,
But wading to the craft, a rusty nail
Impaled my foot, which crimson swam around...

The men sifted the shallow depths, the sand,
Lifted the faded wood, all spatter'd red.
The letters 'VEI'could be discerned:
Twas as if some ethereal, angry hand

Descended 'pon my head, and as it smote,
The watchers saw my body stripped to th'stem;
Restored, retarded, mangled in the boat-
Exact in frame and face as each of them.

Wasteland
Andrew Jagger

There is no beauty at all
to this godforsaken land.
It has tangled trees,
where the branches
sprout plastic shopping bags.
Once there was a pavement,
now there lies a tangled mass
of withered grass.

Here, the lord of the land
is a mangy old cat.
He strides without peer
among the twisted piles of scrap.
This feline dines well,
on a cuisine made up of rats.
Even owning his own palace,
which, many years ago
was someone's trusty vehicle.

The awesome forces of nature
have won this particular battle.
They have reclaimed their land
from the burgeoning grasp of man.
However, like all savage wars,
there is a high cost.
For this once pleasant ground
is now permanently scorched.
Pure innocence,
that is now forever lost.

The Eclipse
Gareth Smith

To me, the gift of light was lost,
Amidst the womb, a bed of frost.
Grown in the dark and kept from view,
I learnt my art. It's name taboo.

To stop the world from rolling round,
I dug my nails into the ground.
The pain held back, my scream a sigh.
The same since birth: too shamed to cry.

The stars they do still glint and gleam,
As relics from some distant dream.
Hanging jewels forever lost,
To chase them down, too high a cost.

But inside, my heart bleeds for change,
To bring those stars within my range.
To live and love at last in peace,
And validate this vain caprice.

And grain by grain the sand does fall,
And change occurs, however small.
This stoic world could be undone,
Sometimes the moon defeats the sun.

Small Orange Glow
Ricky Kane

Radiant orange glow that lights up the moment. Romantic.
The draw of oxygen increases the glow.

Ultimate accessory to your glad glad glad rags. Glamorous.
The draw of oxygen increases the glow.

Breathe in the high and it relaxes with class. Necessary.
The draw of oxygen increases the glow.

The glow of cancer as your life
burns to a butt.

Paula

Jean Trevett

Recognise and reflect,
It's a face we should respect,
Though I suspect,
We don't mirror her at all.
Turn your back and she is gone,
High heels and party all night long.
You're wrong,
She's still hanging on the wall.
We can't hide from rewind,
Play it over in your mind,
Search and find,
Freeze frame, happy times.
Everyone's a user,
Take from me, I'll get from you sir!
Loss is just the start,
Of something else that's new.
Every soul is fed,
With memories of the dead,
Which makes living bitter sweet,
Until it's time to meet.
Each twisted path to take,
Though not for pity's sake,
It's for learning,
From the errors that we make.
Tears to take the blame,
The anger and the shame,
Paula, pretty Paula,
Only time will heal the pain.

Dancing Hasbeens
(The ballad of Rose and Ern)

Carlton Hunt

It's the end of a wet summer season,
She painted her lips on, he polished his slip-ons,
One last turn, strictly for old timers'sake
Fifty years with numbers on their backs,
Not a single mistake.

Her smile would deepen while sewing on the sequins,
His iron depresses the creases on her dresses,
With one ear on the boxing and one eye on the music,
The gliding handsome twosome move now,
Too slow, slow, quick.

In the final holiday ballroom thriller,
Playing up to the driftwood flotilla,
He squints, and can still see her,
Shimmering, out beyond the closed down pier.

They're the dancing has-beens,
The local paper king and queen,
The island's loveliest, loneliest pairing,
Let's hear it for the parquet-flooring darlings.

Come dancing my love.

Windmills

Yvette Hawkins

Like an ever dying flame
Cold hands shelter
From the storm
Like an insecure child needing
Mother and her warmth
Fragile eggshells on the carpet
Roll onto an ice cold stone
An albatross sleeps hovered
Never one to place a home

Like old news wrapped up in
Flavour of the vinegar and salt
Walking down by the brewery
To recall the smell of malt
Ripples in the water
Ever never are the same
Ever never are alike
Since before we heard your name

You were nothing. We were nothing
But everything was new
There is no justification
For me for us for you
There is only but a memory
Some are captured in a frame
Not quite right
Never alike
Since before we heard your name

Like a storm inside an hourglass
Bulletproof within without
Like the music in an elevator
Spinning in our minds
An open book
An open cry
Searching for new rhymes
I'm the dreamer
You're the drifter
Never one to maintain the game
Seasons turning
Children learning
Yet you remain the same
Seasons burning
Children turning
Yet you remain the same.

Walking

Yeti Lee

I'm walking through crowds of people passing other ways
Waterloo Street
Next to where we'd go to see the man and his
saxophone.
He sat outside the jazz café because he
Thought he might play there one day.
The old man who had one leg longer than the other.
Or perhaps he only had one foot?
No one ever stopped to ask.
We'd watch him cleaning car windows for a fiver
Limping around on one black stump shoe
The other faded grey.
No one ever stopped to ask.

Indie girl like a porcelain doll
That we were afraid to touch
Staring back at us with cold eyes
Keeping us distant in case
We break her china skin.

The rains come and an ocean mist
Sweeps above us as
We drink tequila at Quayside monuments.
Then as the day turns grim
Walking back up "that" hill
Creating an "imaginary rope" that is
Necessary for us lazy folk.

I'm walking through crowds of people passing other
ways
And they all recognise me.
Some remain silent
But I can still see their eyes on me as if they know.
Or want to know.
Me.
I'm walking
I'm walking .. Trying not to see
I'm walking
I'm walking .. Trying not to be
I'm walking,.

The sky turns grey
Just as it always does
And monuments and angels remain silent
Not knowing what to say
Even if they could talk.
Passing without thought
Looking
Wandering

Wanting somehow
To create a legend just
So it appears more mysterious
But it never does.
Cold stone on a winter's morning
Cold stone everywhere.
I'm walking through crowds.
Crowds of people
Passing other ways
Crowds of people
Uncertain half smiles,
Half wanting
Something
Anything
They're not sure even exists.

They see me of course
They see me.
Sometimes they carry on walking
Sometimes they smile
(Just like they should)
I'm walking
Not stopping … never stopping
I'm walking.

The Fly

Michele (Sunshine) Schofield

Margaret is a girl of sorrow,
For from the nurse she had to borrow, some fly spray for the room.
The windows were shut and so was the door,
As we prepared for all out war,
And said " Fly prepare to meet thy doom!"

The fly looked down, and suddenly he caught a little whiff,
He buzzed and sneezed, flew around, and then began to sniff.
In vain he tried to fly, but could not anymore,
And as he cried out in his anguished pain,
He dropped towards the floor.

We crowded around our victim, lying there so sad,
And laughed and jeered at the victory, that we had just had.
Above the room was one more fly, and four of the little ones too,
Crying out in their sad voices, "What are we going to do?"

"For without Dad, we all feel bad and might as well be dead,
So let us fly into the spray and follow him instead".
So down they came into that deadly spray, and breathed it deep inside.
They knew that this would be the end,
And they'd die where their Father had died.

Ode To Vic

John J. Whitmarsh

He walked along the London street
With a briefcase in his hand,
And passed along the thoroughfare
That bares the name of 'Strand'-

Every day he passed that way,
A bowler on his head;
Then suddenly he ceased to come -
Old Vic, it seemed, was dead!

They tell of how his end did come
One chilly winter's morn
When he paid his pennies for 'The Times'
And found that it was torn.

In a rage for every jag-ripped page
He swore and stamped and cursed,
Offered to fight the newsvendor man
And sadly came off worst!

Old Vic, in anger and in pain,
Stormed off, yet knew inside
That his battering and torn newspaper
Had put an end to all his pride.

He stood upon old Tower Bridge
And saw, so far beneath,
The water that would be his grave
And knew his dying would be brief.

He dived and died that winter's morn
And the crowd that watched was thick -
And they applauded as he hit the Thames
And saw the last of Vic.

So when you cross the Tower Bridge
And stop upon that road,
Remember what you read right now
Is City Vic's own ode.

A compleX simplicity

Ricky Kane

..seems simple enough?

a friend...
(a female)...
but just a friend
(nonetheless)

a lesser friend...
(more a lover)...
but not an X-friend
(so I hope)

an X-friend...
(though an XXX lover)...
but I can live with that
(no problem)

now an X-XXX lover...
(though an X-X-friend)...
means we're friends again
(at least I think?)

an X-everything...
(can't be good)...
X-friend, X-XXX lover
(X-person)

..when put like that it seems quite complicated?

.

OVER THE FENCE
John Whitmarsh

"Aye, Mrs Jones, it's true what you say,
I have to do it three times a day.
As soon as I've finished and got myself dried,
I'm at it again!" Mrs Brown cried.

"He thinks I enjoy it; well, perhaps I did once,"
She breaks off for a moment, for another peg hunts.
She fills the last inch of the long washing line,
Then rabbits again, "Yes, once it was fine.

But not any more, I'm getting too old;
The interest I had has gone and got cold.
It's nothing to me, no, not any more;
Just another old chore, another old bore.

But Jack'll be home soon, I really must rush,
And give my grey hair a flick with a brush.
Got to get in and get my man fed."
"Aye, Mrs Brown, then drag him to bed."

MISSING
Ken Vater

Mum and dad had several tries
But never see things eye to eye
When left alone, they merely fight
Sometimes it seems to last all night

One morning I came down the stairs
To find my mother sitting there
Her eyes where red, and full of tears
Yet the smile said, have no fear

Although dad's gone, who knows where
There's bits of him here and there
In a chair was one odd sock
I wonder if dad's learnt to hop

We haven't seen dad for awhile
Yet mum is coping, that's her style
So when he came the other day
I smiled hello, and walked away

"Embraced of the night"

Lorna Marshall

Day goes night comes, the light of the moon
shines in through a small opening of the curtains
lighting a small corner of my room
almost taking away my gloom
shadows dance as the wind blows
leaping and jumping like dancers on a stage
I watch the shadows wishing that i one day could
be as free to move so elegantly
but alas, this will never be as they
like me
are only temporary.

MANS INHUMANITY TO MAN

Ron Miller

Since time began it has been their home,
A place where they were free to roam,
Content to live life at their own slow pace,
Not trying to keep up with the rest of the human race.

But now as logging destroys the forests,
And the people of the world, who are the poorest,
They have no hope now, unless it's stopped,
Because by the days, the hours, the minutes, more
trees are dropped.

Their numbers cut, they will soon be destroyed,
Perhaps someone will see why they are annoyed,
They have no weapons to defend themselves,
They only asked to be left in peace nothing else.

When the trees have all gone, and the forest are bare,
There will be nothing left for them, in this world to
share,
Mans inhumanity to man to this day is still rife,
Take away the forests and you take away their life.

Dedicated to the Purnan Tribe, Sarawak

ALGVIRA

Jason Huggett

I am Algvira,
Standing in full battle gear some forty paces,
Between two armies.
They await the signal - the signal from me.
The sign to kill.
To run running, screaming to die.

The clashing of swords,
Thump of body against shield a thousand time;
Slices and slashes and stabs.
Screams.
Screams and shrieks,
And gargling giggles.
Crunching of bone.
They await my signal;
The tearing of flesh.

They expect me.
They assume.
They presume.
They await their signal,
They await their doom.
For a knife I must plunge into the earth,
They wait.

A calm descends as the wind drops,
I fill my lungs with a last breath of life.
My scream a shock wave that rocked the earth,
heard where no sound could be heard,
In the souls of men,
Where I must now put my trust.

My life song of pain and anguish,
And loss and love,
Till the veins in my face and neck,
Pulsed and spasmed.
And with my every breath spent
I ran the blade across my throat.

The spray of blood spilled in a wide arc,
I uttered not a sound
but the fall of my body
on knee and then side
as between the blood soaked grass
I took my last look
through mortal eyes.

Arctic Thaw

John J. Whitmarsh

Block by block,
You have built me an igloo:
It is fashioned from cold sentiment,
From an icy stare,
From your frozen ambitions –
And it has foundations set
In the permafrost of a loveless marriage.

I have walked barefoot these long months,
Waiting at tables in downtown diners
While you awaited my weekly handout;
And you repaid me, ever more often,
With a slap,
With a kick,
Or with closed eyes
That were colder than snow.

But what you cannot know
(The secret that is hidden in my chill)
Is that the signs of a thaw
Are everywhere. They are in my lightened step,
In my fresh-plaited hair,
In the way I smile when your glacier
Face is turned away,
Or when your chemical friend seduces you.

If that is all you have to offer –
A vacant look, a far-off smile –
Then my waiting days are over.
No Arctic spring could ever be as welcome
As the warming glances and melting words
That come on the tide
From the table in the corner –
Block by block, he melts my igloo,
And releases me from my long, dark night.

The Musician

Yvette Hawkins

There is nobody to justify this crescendo
We'll sleep on textile mounds
On broken bottle tops and old garden gate fences
Stencilling our lives in and around
And about the way our dreams have moulded us.

The rush.
Tingling sensations in our toes and noses
And our abdomens
(That's my very own secret)
I've kissed you goodnight
And I'll never forgive myself.

Spinning rounds
Swimming red liquid in emotions
On the floor
I'm spinning
I'm swirling
I can never stop

My heart beats hard
Beats fast
And I'm tired.
Sometimes I give into you
And I'll never forgive you for that.

You are my secret drug
The disease will claim me someday
Psychedelic pictures accompany you
They'll be the death of me too.
I fall with you hard and fast
Remembering only in slow motion
We only have ourselves to forgive for that.

Marmalade For Lions
MIGUEL ANGEL

Faster, lions ran faster
though there was no easy escape.
forests brought demons out their bodies
like it does cranberry marmalade.
They all forgot about their courage
they all wanted to be first
but when you are born a lion
something else runs through your veins.

Faster they ran, almost unstoppable
laws are better obeyed, when overseen
in my mind, they had committed no crimes
but still they ran, as if in need.
I like them when on display
I like them when they are in a cage.
It is just like the taste that's sinful
of sweet cranberry marmalade.

Daydreamer
Lorna Marshall

Sitting here with this puzzled look
Gazing at the white board
Words appearing then being erased
Words spoken but never heard

Daydreaming
Visions of white beaches
Blue clear seas
Dolphins leaping
That's where I would rather be
This feeling makes me so happy

The bell goes my dream disappears
Content as I leave the room
Over come by the feeling of freedom
Walking home I look at the clouds
Each one a different shape
I daydream once more
Finding myself stood at my door
I reach for the key, it glistens in the sun

On entering the house I hear the call of my mother welcoming me home
Climbing the stairs is a mountain the top seems so far away
The bag that clings to my back so heavy yet light
Full of books and memories of the days past events
The day drifts on but I can't seem to get away from day dreaming
With every awaited breath I dream some more.

Love

Lighting Candles

Alan Corkish

why did you light candles for me?
it seems now a pointless exercise
and why did i light candles for you?
they light candles for the dead don't they?

maybe, each in our own way,
we knew it couldn't last
so prepared ourselves in advance
for the inevitable...
a sort of rehearsal
for mourning

...now, here, today, when i light this candle
you will never know it even existed
the Church will be a quid richer
and the people passing will think
that someone died
they'll never guess that this one's for
something that died unnaturally
something smothered prematurely
a pagan and passionless sacrifice
offered on the altar of

The Family

Hurting. Flirting. Cursing.

Yvette Hawkins

These dirty streets have stained my name
My hands hold blood inside a jar
I meant to meet you
I passed you in the car that
I bought with
The endowment I thought I'd
Put away for a rainy day
The rains upon us we
Stick to each other with
Morning sweat
We stick to each other
And peel away.. Hurting.

Once.
Not so long ago when I was new
And you cared just enough to
Speak your mind
I'd save your kisses and keep your
Blood in my jar
And wake through morning seeping
Through fragile curtains
Stuck to you
I'd be stuck to you
And I'd keep you there flirting.

I'd left you sleeping
Fraying from cups of tea and morning toast
I'd left to return to my charcoal streets
And broken alleys
My world you can never control
You wake slowly only with
Fragments of me inside your mind
Inside your mind
Inside your head
Cursing.

What do You Mean

Michele Schofield

By the glow of the moonlight
With aura of dreams
You whisper I love you,
And I ask what it means.
Do you laugh at my wit?
Or admire my charms?
Is it proudness you feel,
As we walk arm in arm?
Then it's infatuation
Or lust that you feel,
And it ebbs like the tide,
As you learn it's not real.
Is it comfort you have,
To have someone there?
A shoulder to cry on,
To know that I care.
This is not love,
You mustn't pretend;
It's nothing but loneliness,
The need for a friend.
Do you stay out of guilt?
Spare me tears as you leave,
Don't confuse this with love,
It's not pity I need!
But can you stand strong,
And never have a doubt,
Or regret was has passed,
When you may go without.
Will you ache for my sorrow?
Live the air that I breath?
Are you willing to die,
To cry when I bleed?
Love is never so simple,
As your words make it seem.
So you whisper I love you,
And I ask.....
What do you mean?

To Touch
E.R.

Through insecurity and fear a mile has entered between us
Our wants and needs have separated us
From ourselves and each other
We are once again individuals rather than 'one'

Maybe this is your time
Maybe this is my time
Yet it is not our time
Take the advantages you've always wanted and be happy

So if we are to be
Our mile will turn into yards
Our yards will turn into feet
Our feet will turn into inches
And
We will touch again

A Piece of You
Gareth Smith 2001

I caught a piece of you,
A moment in your life,
It felt like destiny,
Loving man. Loving wife.

I sealed this piece of you,
In a handful of words,
I spoke them to the air,
The flowers and the birds.

I loved this piece of you,
Yet never saw you whole,
Never saw through your eyes,
Into your tender soul.

I broke this piece of you,
And found another view.
So caring and so strong:
Complete, Beautiful, You.

Love
Helen Parkes

The love that pounds,
for that life waiting for me.

The love that bounds my hands -
and gags my mouth.

The love that burns inside,
and tears my heart in two.

The love from which I hide,
as I hide my love from you.

My Lover's Arms
Sarah Tracy

Nestled gently in my lover's arms
Misty shower of tender kisses
Soothe and awaken with velvet touch
"Arise, my Lady, come to me."

Unleashed, newborn, aching to grow
I reach out, searching urgently
The haven I sought in his arms
"Hush, my Lady, I am here."

Emotions deepen and overwhelm
Soft dewy teardrops, my heart ablaze
Swaying to music unheard before
"Fly, my Lady, take my love."

Floating, flying, my wings are strong
Reaching the impossible height
Soaring higher and higher
"My Lady, be mine."

Waves of eternal peace
Flowing through us
Melting our mortality
Bearing our soul to love
"I love you my Lady."

BROTHERS
Simon Helps

I watched the colour leave your eyes.
Leeched by tears and all the lies, I told.
I did my share of crying to,
And never spared a tear for you,
but I'm sorry and I don't want to be alone.
So If you can forgive me for just one second,
We will be brothers forever.

THE SILENCING OF THUNDER
John J Whitmarsh

For you,
I will achieve the impossible:
I will steal the night,
I will silence thunder,
I will tame the butterfly
I will trap a shadow,
I will catch the wind,
I will hold a river in my hand:

Because
You will hold a river in your hand,
You will catch the wind,
You will trap a shadow,
You will tame the butterfly,
You will silence thunder,
You will steal the night,
You will achieve the impossible
For me.

.

FROM LOVE
Derek Batchelor

What more could please, enthrall, deserve
Of love…so small yet mild,
Can no way word yet so command
Mere minutes born….a child.
So helpless yet form healthy lungs
It's needs somehow are clear,
It's wet it's hungry, has maybe wind
Deciphered from wail and tear.

Incredible view this…perfect replicate
As yet, so small in size,
Fingers and fingernails, even it's toes
Sparse hair with…deep blue eyes.
Enjoying for years it's …angelic ways
Resembling of cherubs above,
This treasure so filling completely our lives
A reward so simply…..'from love'.

SEPARATION
John J Whitmarsh

And now I am back to where
I must share my empty cell
With the ghosts of a thousand others who
Have lives as desolate as mine.
Doing time, a stretch in solitary;
But do not pity me, for I have
Lived through it all before
And somewhere, out there,
A cellmate or a soulmate is waiting
To bend back the bars and
Release me from my isolation.

TEMPEST OF PASSION
Dr.Nilanshu Kumar Agarwal

Nasdaq index has dipped.
The body tempraturee has risen.
Imbalance between celcius and Fahrenheit has generated the heat.
My soul is anaemic
With the fury of sex.
My mind meditating on female body
My whole endeavour to influence the fairsex
My heart pinning
To be the peer of nudity
Nasdaq index has dipped.
No sign of bullish trend.
Only the howling cries of bears.
Hey,Bulls come and oust this bear
Invading the stock-exchange of the soul.

Union Carbide pollutes the natuare.
Pangs of womanhood make me totter.
Deforestation creating ecological imbalance
Her tender skin and ravishing beauty make me lose my patience.
My mind doomed to a certain death
My soul not hearing the song celestial
My voice unable to pray
My breathing system disturbed.
O Bosnian Serbs! do not cleanse the Muslim populace
Rather,come to this territory of my heart
And indulge in the act of purgation.
O Serbs,come immediately
Else my Divinity
Will find it difficult to face my passion.

A Reassurance
S. A. Todd

My love, I think you carve for me a niche
To hide me from the doubts that nightly tax,
And crumple surer thoughts in paper minds.
Vex not your spirit! No force to unleash
Can place so great a rock upon our backs
It cannot be removed by Father Time;
Nor is there any weapon man can make
to blind our eyes, for we are steel and lace;
Beauty on Strength. Truth always lives as long
as falsehood's fickle tongue finds words to break
Barriers of weak trust in inner space.
So shall the stuff of storms and dreams live on
To brace the battling hearts like you and me.
Remembering those like us who are gone:
Encased in flesh, 'til Angels set them free.

Words
David Broome

Where words come from

You led me to your garden, and let me in
I walked to the centre, and stood amazed
Each flower a word

I knelt and touched the flowers, and they spoke to me
I stood, and gasped at the variety of flowers, of words
There was no need to find these words, they were all there
Poetry for you, is not creation, just selection.

This small bloom to my left said beauty, as my finger brushed a petal
A lily at its side, whispers warmth, to my touch
And the rose........love.

There may be other gardens, in other lands, belonging to other people
Do they also speak?
Perhaps they do, but there is no one there to listen

Or maybe the words are spoken so softly, they are missed.

So, why when I hold you, having walked in that garden, can I not express
myself to your full worth?

For You.

LET ME IN

Paul White

Lifting feeling
On the ceiling
Makes my life
The more appealing
Says to my mind
Voice like thunder
"Lift me up
Or drag me under!"

Close inspection
Revealing tension
My fragile mind
Too warped to mention
Leaves me naked
And defenceless
Drug me up
And beat me senseless

Pleading, pleasing
Tempting, teasing
Cut me up now
I think I'm bleeding
Pleasure takes me
Rape and plunder
Letting go
Be torn asunder

Watching waiting
Dehydrating
You know by now
That I'm your plaything
Leaves me sane then
Wrapped in clover
Let me in
And take me over...

SWAYED

Paul White

Who'll put out the fire
When the fire's out of control?
Who'll wonder of guilt
When the guilt's locked up at home?
Who'll forgive our sins
When I can't see we've sinned at all?
Who knows what might happen
If we spent the night alone?

Your Paste and Copy Girl
Sarah Tracy

From behind the Page 3 girl,
I try to catch your eye.
She doesn't really love you!
Her come-on's just a lie!

The hot and sexy stories,
In the girlies - they're not true!
They were written by some old hacks,
Not real lover's like us two.

So read my words and copy them,
Paste them on your heart.
Save the texts and cherish them,
They're for real for a start!!

But, don't settle for the words alone,
They are really not that much,
If they take the place of me,my love
And the loving, human touch.

Eventually they will fade my love,
The pages, torn and old.
The beauty that was in them,
Will soon seem dead and cold.

But here's a heart that's vibrant!
My arms so warm and true.
Thoughts of love abound here,
And the words are just for you.

My Heart, Invert
Gareth Smith

Through muddled eyes you looked at me,
No inner light, no hidden glee.
These warring feelings on your face,
Just pain and grief and loss of place.
When arms reached out to hold my form,
My shining sun gave way to storm.

And so it transpires from this dawn,
No child of love but worthless spawn.
This squandered sperm that spoke too much,
Now shies away at human touch.
I've known from all my years of hurt,
To hold my thoughts; my heart, invert.

The abyss stretched too deep, too fast,
No leap of faith; the void, too vast.
Trapped in shadows beneath my bed,
My fate is sealed. The cage: my head.
And still your voice keeps me here,
To live in death, a frozen tear.

Romantic Moment

Andrew Jagger

How could I show I loved you?
I would take you
on the trip of a lifetime to sunny Florida.
Watching the tides
roll in on a sun-drenched beach.
Just the two of us alone,
that would so romantic do you think?

I can see us passionately embracing
on that beach. There is silence,
except for those waving tides crashing
and raking against the sandy shore.
What need would there be
for any emotive words?
We would already know that
we love each other.

We would still be there
at nightfall, watching the sun
roll down towards the reflecting horizon.
And as the light fades away
from our squinting eyes
our love would not disappear.
Although we should be consumed
by the engulfing darkness,
we instead would burn ever brighter.

silly things

RonMiller

Splashing in the puddles,
Lying on the grass to look at the stars,
Playing in the autumn leaves,
Following a love that leaves no scars.

Doing silly things together,
With the one I love,
Watching people as they stare,
Eyebrows raised, oh heavens above.

Running through a cornfield,
Hand in hand as we jump over waves,
Just living for today,
Lying together in an empty cave.

Sitting on the veranda,
Watching the autumn sun rise,
A blanket wrapped around us,
As we look into each other's eyes.

All these things I'd like to do,
Not just be able to dream of,
And I'm sure that one day it will happen,
When I find the one I love.

My Sons
Samantha Jones

Weep only for a moment ... for I will not leave your side
I am in everything you do, across this great divide
Fear not my sons ... be brave and strong, my heart it cries for you
The rains that gently fall to earth, are tears that I shed too
I am the rippling seashore, perhaps the gentle breeze
Listen and you'll hear me, as a whisper through the trees
So when you weep, weep not for long, my spirit now is free
And I will be your guiding light, throughout eternity

1998 in memory of Diana (Queen of hearts)

"Each beat of my heart is for you"
Derek Batchelor

When I look at my life I see a wonderful place
a place truly full and abound,
It is there everyday, in the smile on your face
and the first time I knew...love I`d found.
The warmth and sensation when holding your hand
and how `special` that way makes me feel,
When so safe and secure your embrace understand
that, the love we both have is....so real.

With merely the prescence of you! in my mind
see these pictures as often before,
You! are these pictures I`d so often find
its the you! that I....love and adore.
At times when my life is so under the weather
when everythings painful and blue,
I have only to touch of the love thats our tether
and all`s well again.....thanks to you!.

You came into my life and nurtured as only
the one of my dreams.....bringing true,
The dream that my heart would...never be lonely
so my first only love...went to you!.
It is only to you! that...I can talk this way
from my heart please believe me...its true,
I know I have hurt you, through tears hope you stay
for my heart loves no other......but you!.

Steeplechase
John J Whitmarsh

Had I the reins of your heart,
I would set you to galloping
All along the chase,
And leaping high fences
In a singular race
Where starting and finishing were
Less important than
A contented smile
And a love-flushed face.

Your blood would pound under my
Crop's ardent touch,
And you would care for nothing as much
As the thrill of the ride
And the wide
Open field.

And you would pant,
Ten times a second,
To feed your tiring muscles -
And you would paw the ground until I beckoned
You over the finishing line,
Then invited you to race
Just one more time.

Had I the reins of your heart,
The season would never end -
And we would chase steeples
Until our hooves wore down.

The Sleeper
Michael Helps 2002

Sunlight pours through net curtains
On this winters day.
Dust floats, sheathed in gold
Like a million angels
Settling on your face.
        You smile
I really should be sleeping
But its worth the wait
To see for just a while.

I catch my breath
Try not to disturb your slumber.
You are the summer
Sleeping through these winter days
And here,
By your side
I'll watch you
And wait…

Luccini
Pete Nightingale

Words flowed,
unceasing,
from your fingers;
became the singers
in my ears.

Luccini
were the bearers
of good tidings;
dissolving
all my fears.

My doubts
you just diverted
to the sidings
of my mind; no longer
were there tears.

Stronger, I became;
and then you wrote:
"I'm leaving." Your legacy:
Luccini. They help me
brave the years.

For Lucy – wherever you are

Our Love
Ron Miller

Life is full of painful surprises,
Illusive visions, shattered dreams,
Feeling bad as love demises,
No crystal clear blue streams.

Love shows itself in many guises,
Sometimes it can seem extreme,
Many colours different disguises,
Enough for everyone it would seem.

But you and me, we gained no prizes,
When our love we confessed,
We were the height of others despises,
We knew our love would not be blessed.

But love is love, without compromises,
We had each other that was enough,
Left alone to our own devises,
Maybe they didn't like it, tough.

The Churchyard
Geoff Hough 2002

We walked round the old Yew-strewn churchyard,
New lovers in that place of ancient sanctuary.
I took you there to reveal myself,
That you could peer into my windowed soul.

Through the gated porch into sheltered haven,
A world apart - we were time spun.

Picking paths through overgrown, untended graves,
Trampling on the past - we were untarnished.

I showed you my patched and ragged church,
Jigsawed in pieces of time - we were whole.

Then tender kissed under deity's tower,
In carefree irreverence - we were ageless.

The Tempest and the Calm

Richard Mccarthy

I don't listen when you call,
I don't buy roses,
nor dress up nice,
Sometimes I am as cold as ice.

I shout and ball and make you cry,
Ignoring pleas for clemency,
I don't cuddle you or hold you tight,
I don't come to bed at tonight.

This angst to you I convey,
Each and every grinding day,
I take no time to stop and wonder,
Of your love for me that I put asunder.

Stop this rage, release me now,
for your love slips from my grasp,
crushed under the weight of words
harsh and jagged like rocks they rasp.

The storm blows over, calm descends,
Relief alround as the tempest fails,
Forgive me my love so soft and fair,
Let gentle breeze now fill our sails.

I love you more than the stars and moon,
And the oceans and the mountains too,
Your eyes like diamonds gleam so bright,
with love and goodness that binds us tight.

Nature

The Quiet Morning
Andrew Shiston

As the mist swirls in the valleys
And drifts across the fields
The ghostly shadows harden
And the ancient trees appear
Old Oaks with giant branches
And waists that span their years
Stand proudly dripping water
From mist as though of tears
In a gentle silent clearing
Between these ancient trees
Stands a broken fallen cottage
Gnarled red ivy round the eves
In this quiet silence of the morning
Before the wakening of the birds
The sound across this clearing
Is the tap tap, tap tap, of water
Dripping down from sodden leaves

Serenade The Trees
Miguel Angel

Listen to the wind through the forest
Looking for somewhere to hide,
From the desperate cries of the city
And the smell of vodka in the night.

As shadows, they become the pathway
That leads the wind to the vast,
It turns away as if knowing,
Hell awaits at the end of the dark.

Then a woman, in naked emotions,
Serenades the trees with her voice,
She lends her passion, as the forest surrenders
As the lover who is never destroyed.

The wind, in exchange, cease her fire,
For it knows she will never be blind,
Of love, when it waits in the darkness
From life which is harder to find.

FINLAND
Andy Saunders

The lighthouse in the distance
Spreads its solemn light;
Waves crash spectacular
Against fools gold spangled night.

Boulders smooth, worn away
As I witness erosion taking place;
Gulls hover still, so graciously
Watching the everchanging face.

Ore stained pools of iron water,
Stagnant little gulfs
Like Poison from a septic wound
As if the World has bled enough.

Magnificense in its splendour
A place that I feel part;
The sea, the sun, the rocks and earth
Are within this very heart.

NATURE'S END
Geoff Hough

Rollered seas break the eternal shore,
Waves that have journeyed ocean reaches,
With one tempestuous finale,
Come to the quieted rest- spent of life.

The raging storm across thundered skies,
With lightening passions in its wake,
Now crushed by efforts existent,
Is suddenly quiescent – drained of force.

Loves laboured journey too,
Turbulent and seldom smooth,
So full of nature's fervent zest,
Oft meets a less than gentle end.
Yet there was a beauty in its passage
And remembrence of togetherness.

But nature does not cease its plan
And as the waves, love will again.

182

"Runt of the litter"
Derek Batchelor

You are the smallest one of eight
where seven are doing well,
Though you...I only sit and wait
as...live or die can`t tell.
You are so very small and weak
just hours into life,
Your chances slim and very bleak
these early days of strife.

Your little body that trembles so
its heart that beats so fast,
You`re fighting hard and this can see
whilst hope your strength will last.
Through every hour I sit with you
and every wish I give,
You`ll fight like hell and then pull through
I want you so ....to live.

My heart goes out to you..mans friend
when nature has her rule,
That live or die we can`t amend
and god....it seems so cruel,
But days have passed and now feel sure
through care you`ll live not fall,
Convinced I am that...when its pure
that love.....will conquer all.

NO SINGLE SOLDIER
Peter Nightiningale

Canto from a foreign shore

The slow, persistent
'shoosh'
of sea on shore,
the almost silent sough;
the dying, sighing cough
as each succeeding
soldier
shudders forth
a final susurration;
then softly slides
beneath the subsequent
shining-strong,
slow-rolling stalwart,
whose last, short-swirling
subjugation
salutes his single,
signal oath:
to sigh – and die –
upon the shingle.
The solemn certainty:
no single soldier
shall survive.

Art

THEM
Nick

Far more than a skirt length
They are her foundation.
Grounding her soul they determine how she stands,
How she carries herself.
It doesn't matter what outfit she wears
If she doesn't know what to put on them.

Generally women are vulnerable when it comes to them.
They are never long enough, never quite thin enough, never quite toned
enough.
But give her a pair of sheer black stockings
And she can carry off anything.
In creating the illusion of perfection you give her confidence in her
sensuality.
What a woman conceals says so much more about her than what she reveals.

Fashion is the exploration of her relationship with her body;
She is what she wears.
The raciness of the short skirt,
The fluidity of the long one,
The modernity of the knee length.
To slit or not to slit;
Each makes a statement that begins and ends with them.

Go into a boardroom and its easy to spot the woman amongst the sea of suits;
The eyes go straight to them.
Put her in trousers and she becomes a different person.
I love the sexiness of her in men's pants,
The street energy of tight faded blue jeans,
Framing her succulent derriere.
Not a question of beauty but of expression
The way she crosses them,
How she gets in and out of a car,
How she looks when she's wearing nothing but a man's shirt.
They have so many facets;
The maternal need of a child clinging to them.
Or the sexual
Sensuously entwined around her lover like a toffee wrapper.

What I love most about them is their movement.
In dance they have the starring role.
Changing character with every stretch and curl,
Each position connects body and soul,
Simultaneously grounding her to earth:
A living work of art

Artistic Vision
Karl Devitt

He talked to me
For just a while
Came inside
Showed himself wide
Revealed his presence
His supreme essence
Purity, let fashion
Showing a side
In my disguise
A face, not wooden
Frozen, capturing vision
Cast in a moment.

Skin
Yvette Hawkins

Shadows crease my skin
A silver tin heart
Hollow
Like seashells on a sandy beach
We're waiting for the moon to rise
And we're only shadows too
Creases in the sea.

Seasonal

SUMMER DAYS

R. J. Miller

Oh those summer days,
The time we spend together is so special,
Your warmth exudes a smouldering passion,
And fills me with the energy of life.

I don't mind that you cannot stay with me,
For I know that the night will be short,
And tomorrow you will return to fill my day,
Your existence burns me through and through.

But when the summer is over,
Your warmth seems to cool,
You return most days throughout the autumn,
But the nights get longer without you.

I can't understand your shyness,
For I still want you as much as ever,
You provide me with no excuses,
As if uncaringly your warmth just cools.

The worst time of all is winter,
For I hardly ever see you,
Life goes from one grey day to the next,
And when you do appear you are cold and distant.

Where are you then, when you are most needed?
Why do you hide yourself away?
Those long cold winter days and nights,
When I need your warmth to surround me.

Spring is such a pleasing time,
When flowers start to bloom again,
As the season gathers pace the days become brighter,
Once again you show yourself as though you never left.

As the weeks pass by you appear more often,
I can feel your warmth growing once more,
This for me is probably the best time of the year,
For I know that you will be with me all summer.

Children on a beach
David Broome

I watch the children in the waves
Delighted squeals and fun
The water rushing in and out
The never-ending sun

Memories of times gone by
This once was me as well
Playing in the sand and sea
That heady seaweed smell

Summers long, ice cream and crabs
I smile as I recall
The simple pleasure once I felt
With bat and net and ball

Am I to old to join the game
Too sensible to stand
Beside these children having fun
With lapping waves and sand?

Christmas 2001
Thomas Moore

Remember Christmas as of old,
white and still, electric cold,
and from the Churches,
loud and clear,
came carols from another year,
but no one seemed to hear.

While in the churchyard, murmuring,
a different choir rose to sing
for those so cosy in their bed,
content, well fed, no fear, no dread,
it sang of scenes so far away,
so far, so far, so far away.

That song was plaintive,wondering,
how can you pray, and play and sing,
while in the distance,wavering,
to those that may be listening,
we all are one how'ere we pray,
so hear us on this Christmas day.

Songs

Dreamwalker
Jörgen Jansson

The thunder-notes entered my head last night
It's that funny accent, the lost voice of Johnny
Was it really you that broke the spell of magic?
Is it really you again from a place in my heart?

These past twenty years I felt a presents close to me
Step up front dreamwalker, let an uncrowned grip your hand
I guess I knew, having a long story with these two souls of mine
Step up front dreamwalker and let us stroll back to mother Ireland

Don't you know you're changing my idea about sanity?
Welcome to the rest of eternity, to my existence
Dreamwalker, you make my heart hit these double beats
Dreamwalker, I'm so pleased we found the beat again

When I was younger, I searched hard to find the answers
And as time went by all these clues turned me deranged
I was reaching the sky above to find strength to carry on
I was laying in loneliness listening for a second heartbeat

When I first realised the truth behind the idea I froze cold
My mixed emotions got me into total confusion about us
How was I supposed to handle these two souls singing high?
How could I know this life wasn't just meant for me alone?

These past twenty years I felt a presents close to me
Step up front dreamwalker, let an uncrowned grip your hand
I guess I knew, having a long story with these two souls of mine
Step up front dreamwalker and let us stroll back to mother Ireland

Don't you know this changed rock'n roll's credibility?
Welcome to the rest of eternity, to the lizzexistence
Dreamwalker, you make my heart hit these double beats
Dreamwalker, I'm so pleased we found the beat again

Love Hurts

Steve Lyons circa 1980.

I love you said the sunrise to the mountains of Ozark
I kiss you every morning till the night do I embark
And when I am not with you I cry with tears of rain
Waiting till the morning and my love to shine again

I hate you said the mountains to the sun above Ozark
For every day you love me and leave me in the dark
And when you are not with me I crack through cold and pain
Waiting for the morning and your love to shine again

Hate me not said the sunrise to the mountains of Ozark
For though I truly love you I must leave you in the dark
I cannot help my actions though I try inane.
You must forever suffer in the wind, the cold, the rain

But I need you said the mountains to the sun above Ozark
You tell me that you love me
Have you ever known the dark
Have you ever sat and shivered in the wind, the cold, the rain
Waiting for the morning and your love to shine again

I love you said the sunrise to the mountains of Ozark
I kiss you every morning till the night do I embark
And when I am not with you I cry with tears of rain
Waiting till the morning for my love
to shine
again

Ballad of the Forty Year Old Man
Paula Cleife

millions of manlets, swimming 'gainst the tide
the 30-something woman wants to be your bride

Can you feel her hunger?
Can you taste her breath?
Does she really want you?
Or are you just the next?

millions of manlets, swimming 'gainst the tide
the 30-something woman wants to be your bride

Is it just a web she weaves?
Emotion's tangled net?
Does she love your body?
Or will she soon forget?

millions of manlets, swimming 'gainst the tide
the 30-something woman wants to be your bride

Are you getting weary?
Are you caving in?
Do you feel your mind is
Wracked with pain and sin?

millions of manlets, swimming 'gainst the tide
the 30-something woman wants to be your bride

What about a lover,
A woman who'se for real?
One who'd love your manlets
Growing slow within?

millions of manlets, swimming 'gainst the tide
the 30-something woman wants to be your bride

Song For Myself
Durlabh Singh

Who am I ?
Someone standing
On the shores
Or some one
Who sailed across
The seven seas.

I am the toiler of sea
A seeder of the earth
An emblem in nectar
For the humming bees
A creator in deeds
For impassioned ends
In tune with liberators.

My organs return to earth
And roads flash under pines
Thrusting the high clouds
To carrying palpitations
Of stilted winds
For some warm season.

Monthly Themed Contests

Februarys Theme
(Poets Over 50 Years)

FIRST PLACE

Celebration
Beth Irwin

Today was a really happy day
A meal, a show, a time to play
Last year I joined Adult Education
I must admit with some trepidation
Never having passed exams before
Nervous as a kitten going through the door
I worried in case they thought me too old
But they all welcomed me into the fold
So now I have some certificates to show
But of course I still have a long way to go
Five Distinctions, two Passes, I am so glad
All in twelve months, So have not done too bad
Two results, I have not yet received
Pass or not, I will still be pleased
Any I failed, I will have another try
Not going to let them pass me by
It is never too late to learn something new
I hope reading this will inspire you too

SECOND PLACE

Peace
Michele Schofield

"Peace", they said,
And gave him toys,
Of soldiers, tanks and guns.
"Tolerance", they whispered,
And showed him how,
Not to love his neighbour.
"Friends", they cried,
"Are all around",
Yet fellowship was not their life.
"Happiness", they hissed,
"Is to be found,
In truth and not hypocrisy".
"Love", they preached,
"Is yours to have,
To keep, to cherish, and to give".
"Peace", they said,
"Is what we want",
And sent him off to war!

JOINT THIRD PLACE

Disco Diva
Samantha Jones

No more disco dancing, no boppin'that's for sure
I tried to do it late last night, ended mangled on the floor
The legs they went all wobbly and me 'ead it still feels numb
I've been stuck here since 3am in agony on me bum
I know Travolta did it and boy did he look nifty
But I should really give it up as I am way past fifty

"Nightmares"
Andrew Shiston

Away out on the starboard beam
Betwixt the stars and earth
Beneath the laden storm clouds
The distant shore lights gleam
The ship that passes on this night
Is a phantom passing through
The wind that whistles in its sails
Is a sailors haunted nightmare
That drives the ship away
He dreams of waves and open sea
Of forever sailing on
Of tempest dark and gloomy depths
Deep sleep far below
To wander in the night
No glance at twinkling lights
Just a phantom passing through....

March Theme
Poems in another language

FIRST PLACE

Anima della luna
©Dragonslayer Tyu 2002

Soltanto,
Potete sentire la mia anima,
Solo,
Potete sentire la mia anima...

Luna,
Voi lucidano con la notte,
Penetrando la nerezza,
Facente il volo dell'introito delle ombre.

Soltanto,
Potete sentire la mia anima,
Solo,
Potete sentire la mia anima...

Chiarire la notte,
Luna giusta,
Lasciarlo vedono i vostri raggi,
Presi in prestito dal sole.

Soltanto,
Potete sentire la mia anima,
Solo,
Potete sentire la mia anima...

Lasciare ombreggia il filtro con la notte,
Dante in su alla luce del giorno,
Nerezza che dà la resistenza,
Luce che li rende deboli.

Soltanto,
Potete sentire la mia anima,
Solo,
Potete sentire la mia anima...

Lasciare la nerezza entrare,
Ostruiscono la luce dalla vista,
Fiducia nella vita che li dò,
Poiché soltanto...
Può sentire la mia anima.

Translation:

Soul of the Moon

©Dragonslayer Tyu 2002

Only you,
Can hear my Soul,
Only you,
Can hear my Soul...

Moon,
You shine through the night,
Penetrating the darkness,
Making shadows take flight.

Only you,
Can hear my Soul,
Only you,
Can hear my Soul.

Illuminate the night,
Fair moon,
Let me see your rays,
Borrowed from the Sun.

Only you,
Can hear my Soul,
Only you,
Can hear my Soul.

Letting shadows filter through the night,
Giving up in the light of day,
Darkness giving strength,
Light making you weak.

Only you,
Can hear my Soul,
Only you,
Can hear my Soul.

Let the darkness enter,
Obstruct the light from view,
Trust in the life I give you,
Because only you...

Can hear my soul.

Amor de mi corazón.
Dave Seaman

Mi corazón es tuyo para siempre,
Y tu corazón es mio para toda la eternidad.
Conozco que eres me una ama verdadera.

Contigo soy siempre felíz;
Mi mundo es completo cuando estoy contigo.
Yo nunca conozcí que es posible a tener amor como esto.

Mi corazon está en tus manos.
En tus ojos veo la significa de la vida,
Dulces sueños tengo ahora.

Mi amor, te quiero ahora y siempre,
Te amor con toda mi alma.
Esta es la dulce vida, amor de mi corazon.

Love Of My Heart
Dave Seaman

My heart is yours forever,
And your heart is mine for all eternity.
I know the you are my one true love.

With you I am always happy;
My world is complete when I am with you.
I never knew that it was possible to have love like this.

My heart is in your hands.
In your eyes I see the meaning of life,
Sweet dreams I now have.

My love, I want you now and always,
I love you with all my soul.
This is the sweet life, love of my heart.

THIRD PLACE

Sublimation : au goût du jour
Eric Truant

Je hume ces moments
où nous sommes là,
comme ça
en face l'un de l'autre
à écouter nos cœurs ;
je te serre contre moi,
comme ça
tu me souris
tes yeux pleins de douceur.

Le temps
semble se suspendre
pour nous deux,
tu me parles
mais je ne vois que tes yeux,
enivrons-nous de ces baisers
que nos bouches réclament
comme l'union symbolique
de nos âmes...

J'embrasse
une à une tes mains,
si lentement,
que j'oublie.
J'oublie
un monde
de violence,
enkysté de folie,
pour m'emplir
de cette volupté
qui te rend femme
lorsque je suis ta bougie,
que tu es ma flamme.

Sublimation: In the style of the day
Eric Truant

I smell these moments
Where we are there,
Like that
Opposite one of the other one
To listen to our hearts;
I curl you up against me,
Like that
You smile to me
Your eyes full of sweetness.

Time
Seem to hang
For us two,
You speak to me
But I only see your eyes,
Let us get drunk on these kisses
That our mouths demand
As a symbolic union
Of our souls ...

I kiss
One to one your hands,
If slowly,
That I forget.
I forget
A world
Of violence,
madness,
To fill me
Of this sensual delight
who makes you a woman
When I am your candle,
That you are my flame.

April's theme
Disability
(Poetry on a disability theme or from disabled poets)

FIRST PLACE

The Whiff of Age
Geoff Hough

Fragrant life that seemed ever long,
Now so vacant and listless born.
When comes youths turn to bitter mellow
And early seasoned sap flavoured sour.

The fiery, sparkled boy of old
Replaced by weary time worn bones.
Heavy- hearted down trod spirit
Where once life's gates hailed open to it.

Longhaired summers a world away.
Ripe futures choice and ready to be plucked.
Now talk is of things that were
And not those beckoning to be.

Those years wished in careless abandon;
Willing the doors of men to open wide.
(Glancing back with laughter),
 That boy wanting, needing to be old.

The pangs and pains of youth forgot.
Life's turns reviewed and weighed for want.
Those family gatherings to celebrate,
Now we only meet to mourn and wake.

Fragrant life that ever was,
For all the suffered age of now,
For all the silent angst and agony:
I have lived, I have loved, I have been.

SECOND PLACE

FEAR!
D.R.Emery

Lost in swirling mind of turmoil,
Which that i could find and not boil,
Concerned of my emotional state,
Feeling apathetic at a pathetic rate.

Emotionaly strung on pressured high,
Fear of losing what I've got , Yes I!
Lonliness is all that i know,
as no one can understand me so:-

I'm angry with my self, troubled with guilt,
My brain is bent, my body wants to wilt,
I want love but can't except i've got it,
Because the mirror only reflect the rot in it,

i feel rejected because i'm down,
I can't swim, I feel i'll drown,
I'm searching very hard for the key here,
But all I know right now is I feel fear!

THIRD PLACE

Electric Schizophrenic
Mike Helps 1998

It was so strange
That they only saw
The light of fluorescent eyes
And the cold steely skin.

Only I seemed to see
The delight of a mechanical smile
And the fact that she lived within.

I felt such a broken fool
Because they laughed
When she ran into the wall.
No-one told her she
Couldn't get over it
So she never stopped trying

Finally, they reset the time
In her tiny electric mind
To awake
When I left
But it was too late.

Because when I touched
Those plastic lips
My tin heart exploded.

May
Five minute poems

FIRST PLACE

The Gift
Paula Cleife

My Sister:
The Gifter.
Honeymoon to relax.

Menorca:
The Daughter
Of Balearics.

We're rested,
Injested
And now we are back.

So grateful
With Caseful
Of Xorigeur and schnapps!

SECOND PLACE

FIVE MINUTES
Pete Nightingale

In your three-score years and ten you will burrow like a mole,
unseeing, through 'five minutes' seven million times.

Your first five minutes are a celebration of your birth;
the last an encapsulation of your death.

Of neither know you little;
now or then.

Of those between, you hold but the slightest recollections -
earthmounds where the mole, for just a moment, breached the surface.

Each an incident significant;
but only by its insignificance.

You burrow blindly through the dark and daylight,
your only long-term goal your death.

How many of your seven million opportunities have you,
truly, given freely, as a gift, to others?

Only you, the reader, can give the honest answer.
For my own part, I am ashamed.

THIRD PLACE

Gone In Just Five Minutes
Ken Vater

To write a poem just for fun,
In pros, in rhymes, and very bad puns.
To write a verse, to quick to last,
There's one minute gone, I must type fast,

What cruel hand invented time,
It's all to short, I'm all behind.
The seconds pass, with galloping pace,
My brains gone numb, the lines erased.

That's two down, just three to go,
What can I write, I wish my clock was slow.
When I'm at work, times a slug.
Yet when I'm home I can't keep up.

Well I'm up to four, and nothings said.
So have I been wasting time instead.
Upon the face these sweeping hands,
To mop the sweat you understand.

With less than sixty seconds left,
This poems dissolved into a mess.
So pray be warned when writing rhyme,
Five precious minutes is no time.

June
Poems About Poets

The Performance Poet
by Yvette Hawkins

A silent poet
A miming poet
A rhyming poet in time
Flying by on random nights with
Damning views on
Political news to
use in elegant prose
I could say
I am one of those.
Here to confess to you
Here to undress with you
Statements never clear
Hidden agendas on
Spoken tenders
Hoping for a career
Hoping I'll still be here next week
Spouting out verse
Shouting unrehearsed
Lines that don't make sense much
Watching you keep your senses in
Alignment.

My assignment -
I'm refining each verse
I'll confide
And politely define each words birth
For you to retrieve
Consume and digest
Until you get bored and go home to your beds
Where you forget all my rhymes
all my rhythm and verse
That I stressed out of sleep
And painfully rehearsed.

I write a new rhyme
That comes to my mind
Out of thinking out loud and
New words that I find in

Torn papers and
Speaking to old strangers I meet
On street corners
Wheeling trolleys of old dollies they keep.
For conversation and tea parties
I rise to my feet..
And quickly run away
These stories I tell and tantrums I yell
Are only here to bemuse you.
Unstructured rhythm that invoke this jism
Can only be to confuse you

On a drunken spell
You may as well
Smile until I've finished.

... No I haven't finished.
So I'll talk about the weather or the
sea for a while
Because thats what poets do
Or I could write about something interesting
But thats when a poets through
When they've lost the inspiration
To ponder lifes wonders
Skim pebbles and stones and
Minute mans blunders
Sipping cofee on continental streets
Tipping Angels and travellers they meet
With proverbs and nouns
Conversation profound
Thinking
Thats the reason why
They were put on this earth.
To make haste with our waste
And ponder our fate
Through a verse,
We choose to contemplate
Leaving questions unanswered.

A beguiled childs laughter
keeps us from this solitude
Exhausted
Converasation chewed
And we resort
To mundane and discipline
Knowing only as humans
We could never win.

So we turn to the heavens on hazy days
And hope for something new
Believing in greater things and
Magical wins
For minds alike to stew
Just like me like you.

I'll write another poem though when
The time is right
That maybe not about ming boggling shite
I'll write a new verse
For you to congest
For you to retrieve
Consume and digest
Until you get bored and go
Home to your beds
Where you'll forget all my rhymes
All the rhythm and verse that I'll continue to
stress out of sleep
And painfully rehearse.

P N

John J Whitmarsh

He is the single soldier
Fighting for the right of words
To tell the tale of
His very human ailment;
A statement,
Short, yet as wide as continents,
Echoes his Blackpool tears,
And names omitted
Confess to sins committed
In the name of – and as a consequence of –
The game of
Life.
Apparent in lines of sweeping verse
Are his loves and losses
And the nature of the crosses
Fate handed him:
But the remembrance of a mother
With her plaintive:
'Please do not forget,'

And a file marked up
'Regret'
Are just the inward parts of him –
At the heart of him
(And not by chance)
Is the poet with a pen
Dipped in light –
Consider the dancing night
With its chimney stacks, and
The nineteen-fifties France
Complete with bats!
Where words of several slivered syllables
March proudly against a prosaic tide
To scythe down hackneyed phrases,
Or when,
In a rush of inspiration,
He goes to clear the outward ground
For fledgling thoughts to sprout
In his readers'buzzing heads,
Can
His artistry be denied
Or his wit or wisdom
Or his fine-tuned ear
Ever be dismissed?
I give you this:
No Nightingale sang sweeter,
Nor a painter ever matched
His ability to snatch
A mirrored scene and keep it.
Be it a lamenter's languished sob
Or laughter's falling tear,
His words make no demands on us
Save those we gladly bear.

Me! A Poet?

Andrew Shiston

Each day comes with passing thoughts
A word a phrase or dream
What's been said to me
Or something that I've seen

Things that I remember well
From past and older times
Things I felt about someone
By touch or by their smell

It's only when you write them down
And put things into rhythm
That what you've finally written down
Could be a peoples poem.

The Poet's Site

S.Tracy and J.Jansson

A roller-Coaster we found from the start,
When we came to this with hope in our heart.
It moved so fast, our head's in a spin,
With poems to write and prizes to win.

Now June's about the poets we like best,
Now, that's a hard one, a real blinking test.
'Cos we love them all, they've served us well,
With the feelings they've shared and the stories they tell.

Now, John and Pete? - They write so well.
And Paula and Dave? - Well they're just swell.
Michelle? Miguel?Where do we start?
They've captured our mind and our heart.

It's not about stanzas and everything neat,
It's about sharing life - that special treat.
Or the pain was too much and you're feeling blue,
But you've shared it, and so, you 've halved it in two.

So it's hard to say who we like the most,
To them all - a glass - and this our toast,
Keep writing, keep sharing, just let yourself go.
Let your soul do the talking and go with the flow.

So, from J and I, we both want to say,
You ahve brightened our life and made our day.
We love you all, 'cos you write from the heart,
And we'll cherish the moments until we must part.

JOINT THIRD PLACE

A Poet By Another Name
Robert Beau

Each poet has a unique way of expressing a feeling or thought
They try not to admonish others or to leave one distraught
As each line or verse unfolds their thoughts are revealed
A message sent is like an unexpected package unsealed
As you extract from their message that which applies
Remember it is about content and not size
Poets may remain undiscovered until they arte rendered to the earth
But they words they have written may affect every birth
Be it from "Trees" that Kilmer once wrote
Or the unnamed author who left just one small note
Take this time to recognize that we are all poets under the skin
It matters not; be we obese or thin
As one's writing may appear shallow to you
Remember we need not be critical of what others do
Your favorite passage may have been words from a poet a long time ago
But their impact may be felt by each person you know

THE PEOPLE'S POET
Dave Brown

Touching folks in verse and rhymes,
She makes us laugh and cry sometimes
And in those lines you really feel
As though you're there, it seems so real.

Some days she writes five or six;
On others none, she needs no fix.
But when mood takes her, quill in hand,
The ink flows quick about car or band.

Red hair, brown eyes, that gorgeous smile:
She's talented and sexy with the right kind of style.
You'll laugh out loud with her fabulous wit
And to me she's always THE PEOPLE'S POET.

And now for the unveiling of our Journal poets collaboration poem.........

THE PEOPLE'S POEM

i
A poem - the song of a seasoned soul,
Reflections of a summer storm
Or a prayer murmured low;
Limitless, but bound with care.

Constructed in a cloistered mind,
But freed, to burst into a million stars -
Which awe the watching populace;
As did one single star.

A soft petal from one of these souls
Whose lives are eternal to live.
Even after, it lies on the ground
Those words exist to set free.

ii
From seeds of thought to a fertile earth
sown to many the heart and of mind,
Hence remaining eternal to inspire exist
for once being is forever entwined.

A heart imprinted onto a page,
open for the world to see.
An expression of affection, and ode to despair,
pure emotion poured out in indelible ink.

A poet never forgets the inspiration for each poem,
each love lost, every happy memory.
A poet's work is his autobiography, written
over the years, each new experience a fresh pen-stroke.

iii
A poem, the life of an inner calling
A mirror of words reflecting the soul
Bearing the needs of a poet's heart
Wishes, thoughts stated for a lifetime.

And the populace waits in anticipation
Till words, ideas, hopes, dreams and fears
Blow their minds, sear their souls and petal their hearts
Until for a moment, or forever, perspectives change and brighten.

Each one sharing that self same goal
Of reaching out with their hearts and minds
To feel every word as a treasured gift
To embrace the world and all of the passion within.

iv
Forgotten ancestors remember us now
As we take an honorable bow
Our innocents remembers thee
However lost remember me.

words in verse
a window of life we traverse
whether mirth or woe
the words from our souls flow

the words envelop; transcends
to a deeper meaning descends
to touch another
exposing raw feeling together.

v

what are words but a spectrum ,whirling round & round,
in a frequencey that we call sound.
for it is music of a different kind,
the shapes you hear are less defined,
they can break your heart or pick on you,
some are false & some are true.

Though thoughts and words of a soul
Reach beyond earth and light
And are beyond reach of mortals,
They are see in the darkness of night
As brightest of comets that score the nights sky,
That tell thoughts and words with tails long and bright
And are seen through optics as streaks of light.

For the word is all the poet has
To punch through the wall of the intangible
Words to tie our existence together
Words to manage the unmanageable
A word can break the camel's back
A word can bring the lover back
A word to find and mend the crack
A word to look for all we lack.

(Geoff Hough, John Whitmarsh, Pete Nightingale, Miguel
Angel Berrios, Derek Batchelor, Dave Seaman, Sarah Tracy, Jorgen
Janssen, Susan Whitmarsh, Samantha Jones, Gareth Smith, Michele
Schofield, Cheryl Cunliffe, Bruce Logan, Andrew Shiston, Scott Tyrrell)

AND FINALLY...
A Dedication Page

I felt that it was important to realize that some of the greatest and most loved poetry is created in the minds of people who suffer a great deal ; not only for their art but for their life in general.. This poem by the innovative poet Alan Corkish, serves as a tribute to the Bipolar Poets.

Damp Friday

Bootle Strand
on a damp Friday evening
not even knowing
why he was there
not at all conscious
of self
until that voice
disturbed then
it flooded through him
and he elbowed through
staring crowds
each step quicker
than the last
and brakes screeched
in the rain
horns blared
in his brain
as he crossed
Stanley Road
seeking shelter
and seclusion
with a child's
concerned phrase
whipping at him
lashing at him
tearing through
his muddied mind;
'Mummy that
man's crying...'

Want to know more? Please see Alan's page on Bipolar online:
http://www.zyworld.com/alanjulia/Alan/bipolar.htm

Authors' Index

Titles' Index

214

ORDER FORM
(copy as required)

SUBSCRIPTION: Quarterly Journals and Christmas Magazine   £12.50

BOOK TITLES:

TPP 2003: In print from mid November 2002 (ISBN 0-954-3621-0-1)
The People's Poet Anthology 2003 (ordered NOV 02-JUN 03)   £6.50
TPP 2003 (ordered from JUL 03 from remaining stock)   £5.00
TPP 2003 (ordered from a new print run after JUN 03)   £POA
TPP 2004: In print from mid November 2003 (ISBN 0-9543621-4-4)
The People's Poet Anthology 2004 (ordered before Nov 03)   £6.00
TPP 2004 (ordered NOV 03 to JUN 04)   £6.50
TPP 2004 (ordered from JUL 04 from remaining stock)   £5.00
TPP 2004 (ordered from a new print run after JUN 04)   £POA
This Is For You (by P Cleife) : In print April 2002   £5.00
TPP Book of Wicked Verse: In print Autumn 2003   £5.00
TPP Book of Love Poetry: In print January 2004   £5.00
TPP MDF Project (as yet untitled): In print Summer 2003   £6.00
TPP Book of Mothers: In print February 2004   £5.00
TPP Book of Goodbyes: In print Spring 2003   £5.00
TPP Book of Muddy Paws: In print Summer 2004   £5.00
TPP Book of Erotic Verse: In print date TBA   £5.00
TPP Tower of Strength: In print date TBA   £5.00
BASIL'S ISLAND: In print date TBA
£TBA
PERSONAL ANTHOLOGY (from the winner of TPP 2002 award...as yet untitled)

COMING SOON:......Funny Verse, a multi-part set including a cd and braille cards, more children's titles and the personal anthology of the TPP 2003 award winner.

✂ ....

Amount Enclosed:

Name: ....

Address: ....

....

email : ....

Cheques payable to: PAULA BROWN
                       10, Enfield Road,
                       Oakdale,
                       Poole,
                       Dorset
                       BH15 3LJ

VOTE FOR THE PEOPLE'S POET 2003 HERE!!!
Official voting form

Name: ....

Address: ....

email : ....

Who is your People's Poet 2003?: ....

Entries must be made on THIS official form only, no copies of any description will be accepted. The nomination must be any poet with work in this book. Anybody may vote ONCE only on this official form.
If you do not want to spoil your book, you will need to buy another one.

✄ -- - -- - - - - - - - - - - - - -

COMPETITIONS:
Design the cover for the 2004 anthology.
Please complete this form and send with your entry. We require a copy or email image of your design. DO NOT send original art at this stage as we can not return entries. You may enter via email BUT you must also send this original form in the post or your entry will be invalid. Original artwork may be required by the printer and you must make it available.

Name: ....

Address: ....

email : ....

Title of artwork : ....

I have read the terms and conditions at www.thepeoplespoet.co.uk and agree to them. I am over 18.

Signature: ....

✄ -- - -- - - - - - - - - - - - - ✄

Annual Themed Contest
EVERYONE IS LOOKING AT ME!!! (This could be anything from your first time on stage, through an embarrassing moment to pure paranoia!)
Poems may be of any length or style.

Name: ....

Address: ....

email : ....

Title of poem : ....

I have read the terms and conditions at www.thepeoplespoet.co.uk and agree to them. I am over 18.

Signature: ....